EAGLES
MASTERPIECES

CRYSTAL PALACE F.C. 1905

Written by Brian Leng
Special thanks to Ian King

A TWOCAN PUBLICATION

©2015. Published by twocan under licence from Crystal Palace FC.

ISBN: 978-1-909872-74-5

1

Memories of certain moments and periods in the club's history are always bought to life for me when I take a look through a book highlighting achievements from different decades and this is a perfect example.

Having supported this club for many years I have had the pleasure to watch some really exciting and entertaining players and this book highlights fifty players who have represented the club.

In our 110 year history we have been fortunate to have some great players and it must have been a difficult decision when it came to deciding who to include but having read the book I must say the publishers have selected an excellent group of players.

As you make your way through you will be able to enjoy not only some great imagery of the players but details of their time playing at the club. This is will rekindle some great memories as the story of their Palace careers are told in this latest book about our club.

I know you will find it an interesting read and, like myself, enjoy a trip down memory lane as Palace masterpieces gives us an opportunity to remember.

Up The Palace.

Steve Parish
CHAIRMAN

FULL NAME:
Darren Paul Ambrose

POSITION:
Midfielder

DATE OF BIRTH:
29 February 1984

PLACE OF BIRTH:
Harlow

CRYSTAL PALACE DEBUT:
8 August 2009

APPEARANCES:
122

GOALS:
35

An outstanding midfielder who was capped by England at Youth and U21 levels, Darren Ambrose was a product of the Ipswich Town Academy, eventually making his debut in League football in April 2002. He soon became an outstanding performer for the Suffolk club and after only 37 appearances he was sold to Newcastle United for £1 million. After two years at St James' Park, Ambrose moved back south to join Charlton Athletic in a £1.5 million move to the Valley that would last four seasons.

It was in July 2009, after a loan spell back at Ipswich Town, that the opportunity to join Palace arose and with his contract with Charlton about to expire he made the move to Selhurst Park on a free transfer. The move turned out to be an excellent piece of business for Palace and for the next three seasons, Ambrose excelled in midfield, as well as weighing in with a few important goals. None more so perhaps, than his strike in a 2-2 draw against Sheffield Wednesday on the final day of the 2009/10 season that helped ensure survival for his team and consign their Yorkshire opponents to relegation.

When his former Ipswich Town manager George Burley took over the Selhurst Park hot-seat in the summer of 2010, Ambrose's future at the club certainly looked secure. However, his first-team appearances under Burley were limited and it was only after Dougie Freedman took over as manager midway through the 2010/11 season that he re-established himself in the side.

AMBROSE

The following season, Ambrose scored one of Palace's greatest-ever goals, a stunning 35-yard rocket in a 2-1 victory over Manchester United at Old Trafford that was voted Goal of the Decade by Palace fans.

His career with the Eagles came to an end during the 2012 close-season, when he was transferred to Birmingham City for a fee reported to be in the region of £250,000.

Ambrose then enjoyed a spell in Greece with Apollon Smyrni before returning to Ipswich for a third spell at the club. He is now plying his trade with Colchester United having signed a one-year contract with the League One club at the start of the 2015/16 season.

Born in Newcastle upon Tyne to an Irish father and a Nigerian mother, Chris Armstrong began his career in league football with Fourth Division Wrexham, making his debut during the 1989/90 season while still a teenager. At the Racecourse Ground he began to show promise as a striker, eventually scoring 13 times in 60 appearances for the Welsh club.

In August 1991, Armstrong moved to Millwall in a £50,000 deal but after only one season with the Lions, he joined Crystal Palace who were in the Premier League at the time.

At Selhurst Park, Armstrongs's career blossomed and in his first season in the top flight he finished as the club's leading scorer with 23 league goals, although this was not sufficient to save Palace from relegation. A live-wire striker with pace, touch and the ability to finish with style, he became hugely popular with the Selhurst Park faithful. However, his goal-scoring achievements in the Premier League's inaugural season had not gone unnoticed and as he continued to find the target regularly in Division One, he began to be linked with a number of top clubs.

A move away from Selhurst Park became inevitable and in 1995, after netting an impressive 58 goals in 136 appearances for Palace, Armstrong joined Tottenham Hotspur for £4.5 million, a club record for the North London side.

His impressive strike rate continued at White Hart Lane and in his seven years at the club he bagged 52 goals in 178 appearances. After a brief spell with Bolton Wanderers, Ambrose returned to Wrexham where he finished his playing career at the end of the 2004/05 season.

FULL NAME:
Christopher Peter Armstrong

POSITION:
Forward

DATE OF BIRTH:
19 June 1971

PLACE OF BIRTH:
Newcastle upon Tyne

CRYSTAL PALACE DEBUT:
2 September 1992

APPEARANCES:
136

GOALS:
58

Mel Blyth holds a unique place in the history of Crystal Palace Football Club having scored the club's first ever goal in English football's top flight, a looping header in the 2-2 draw against Manchester United at Selhurst Park in August 1969.

FULL NAME:
Melvyn Bernard Blyth

POSITION:
Defender

DATE OF BIRTH:
28 July 1944

PLACE OF BIRTH:
Norwich

CRYSTAL PALACE DEBUT:
First: 10 August 1968
Second: 12 November 1977

APPEARANCES:
254

GOALS:
12

Born in Norwich, Blyth began his career at Carrow Road, but only made the breakthrough into first team football after joining Scunthorpe United early in the 1967/68 season. A year later, after seeing United relegated to Division Four, Blyth was signed by manager Bert Head and soon became an almost permanent fixture in the Palace side.

Initially signed as a wing-half, he soon proved his worth as a solid central defender, forming a formidable partnership with John McCormick. In his first season at Selhurst Park, he helped the club clinch promotion to Division One and whilst the years that followed in the top flight were invariably ones of struggle, Blyth was rarely out of the Palace side.

The club's stay in the top league ended in 1973, the beginning of an alarming slide that saw them slip down another division a year later. Blyth spent a long time on the treatment table during this period and following the arrival of Ian Evans from QPR, he was transferred to Southampton for £60,000.

Under new manager Lawrie McMenemy, Blyth enjoyed one of the best spells of his career and was voted Player of the Year by Saints' supporters in his first season at the club. Then, in 1976, he was a key member of the Southampton side that lifted the FA Cup after beating Manchester United at Wembley.

His career at the Dell came to an end in 1977 and after a brief spell back at Palace, he finished his top-class playing career at Millwall.

BACK L-R: John McCormick, Alan Birchenall, John Hardie, John Jackson, Mel Blyth, Gerry Queen.
MIDDLE: Alan Pinkney, David Payne, Peter Wall, Steve Kember, Phil Hoadley, Bobby Tambling, Terry Wharton.
FRONT: Terry Long (trainer), Tony Taylor, Gerry Humphreys, John Loughlan, Jim Scott, Bert Head (Manager).

CRYSTAL PALACE, JULY 1971

FULL NAME:
Yannick Bolasie

POSITION:
Midfielder

DATE OF BIRTH:
24 May 1989

PLACE OF BIRTH:
Kinshasa, DR Congo

CRYSTAL PALACE DEBUT:
25 August 2012

APPEARANCES:
120

GOALS:
8

CORRECT AS OF 17 OCTOBER 2015

Born in Kinshasa, DR Congo, Yannick Bolasie was only seven months old when his family moved to England. Brought up in Lewisham, Bolasie signed for Rushden & Diamonds at the age of 16, but his stay with the Conference side lasted little more than a few months, when he decided to try his luck in Europe with Maltese Premier League side Floriana.

In 2008, Bolasie returned to England and joined Plymouth Argyle, although his first league appearance was during a loan spell with Barnet. He went on to make over 50 appearances for Argyle, before joining Bristol City in 2011, where he picked up the club's Young Player of the Year award, at the end of his first season at Ashton Gate. However, Bolasie's desire to return to London persuaded him to submit a transfer request during the 2012 close season and soon afterwards he moved to Selhurst Park, signing a three-year contract for an undisclosed fee.

Bolasie made his Palace debut in a Championship game at Middlesbrough at the start of the 2012/13 season and was virtually an ever-present thereafter, his exciting and creative wing play making him a great favourite with the Palace faithful. The campaign saw the Eagles secure promotion to the Premier League via the Play-Offs, although Yannick was an unused substitute in the 1-0 victory over Watford in the final at Wembley.

BOLASIE

To cap a great season for Bolasie, international recognition arrived in March 2013, when he made his full international debut for the Democratic Republic of Congo in a goalless draw against Libya in a 2014 World Cup qualification game.

FULL NAME:
Yannick Bolasie

POSITION:
Midfielder

DATE OF BIRTH:
24 May 1989

PLACE OF BIRTH:
Kinshasa, DR Congo

CRYSTAL PALACE DEBUT:
25 August 2012

APPEARANCES:
120

GOALS:
8

CORRECT AS OF 17 OCTOBER 2015

Bolasie's baptism in Premier League football came in October 2013 in a disappointing 3-1 defeat against Liverpool at Anfield, but he fared much better when he returned to Merseyside almost a year later to score his first top-flight goal in a 3-2 victory over Everton at Goodison Park. Later that season, he became the first Palace player to net a hat-trick in the Premier League, an amazing treble scored in the space of just eleven minutes against Sunderland at the Stadium of Light.

Bolasie was selected for the 2015 Africa Cup of Nations in Equatorial Guinea and was on target in the 1-1 draw against Zambia, in the Democratic Republic of Congo's first group game at the Nuevo Estadio de Ebebiyin. Congo went one down after only 62 seconds, when Zambia's Given Singuluma netted, but just after the hour mark, Bolasie equalised in style from just inside the area.

In September 2015, with rumours of a possible move to one of the Premier League's top clubs beginning to circulate in the media, Bolasie ended the speculation and pledged his immediate future to Palace by signing a new three-and-a-half-year contract, much to the delight of everyone at the club.

"Yannick is an exciting player, a talisman for the club in some ways and someone who has been with us a while now," said co-chairman Steve Parish, "I'm very pleased, as is our manager Alan Pardew, that he's still a Palace player,

BOLASIE

because it's not all about buying players, but also keeping the good ones we've got. The manager was very clear on who his key players are, and Yannick is someone we'd love to keep at the club for a long time."

FULL NAME:
Mark Abraham Bright

POSITION:
Forward

DATE OF BIRTH:
6 February 1962

PLACE OF BIRTH:
Stoke-on-Trent

CRYSTAL PALACE DEBUT:
15 November 1986

APPEARANCES:
286

GOALS:
113

Born in Stoke-on-Trent, Mark Bright initially worked in a factory while playing part-time for Leek Town in the Cheshire League. He went on to join Port Vale in 1981, having previously been released from their youth team a few years earlier at the age of 16.

Bright made his first-team debut for the Valiants towards the end of the 1981/82 season, but it was following the arrival of John Rudge as manager that he really came to prominence at Vale Park. The 1983/84 season saw Bright net ten goals in 31 appearances, but having turned down a new contract, he was then sold to First Division Leicester City for £33,333.

His stay at Filbert Street was relatively short and in November 1986 he was signed by new Palace manager Steve Coppell for a fee of £75,000. At Selhurst Park he lined up alongside Ian Wright to develop what was soon to become, arguably the most lethal striking partnership in the club's history.

In the two seasons that followed, the Eagles came close to reaching the promotion Play-Offs with Bright 's 24 goals in the 1987/88 campaign, winning him the Golden Boot for the highest scorer in the Division. Promotion was finally achieved the following season after a third-place finish had secured Palace's spot in the Play-Offs. Bright was on target in the semi-final win over Swindon Town, which was followed by a 4-3 aggregate victory over Blackburn Rovers in the final, to secure the return of top-flight football to Selhurst Park.

BRIGHT

The 1989/90 season saw Palace consolidate their position in Division One, due in no small measure to Bright 's twelve goals which helped to earn him the club's Player of the Year award.

The campaign is perhaps best remembered for a stirring run in the FA Cup that saw Palace reach the final eventually losing in a replay to Manchester United. The Eagles semi-final victory over Liverpool has gone down as one the club's greatest-ever performances, and Bright's thunderous goal in the dramatic 4-3 victory is certain to live long in the memory of Palace fans.

The following season saw Palace finish third in the league, the highest in their entire history, with Bright netting an impressive sequence of seven goals in ten games over the Christmas period. Between them, he and Ian Wright were now regarded as the finest striking partnership in the English game, which was perhaps never better demonstrated than in the 8-0 demolition of Southend United, when both players netted hat-tricks!

Even after Wright moved on to Arsenal, Bright continued to find the target and his record of 17 goals in the 1991/92 campaign was the highest ever achieved by a Palace player in the top flight. His career at Selhurst Park, that had seen him net an impressive 113 goals in 286 appearances, finally came to an end in September 1992 when he moved north to join Sheffield Wednesday.

By then he was thirty years old, but soon demonstrated that he had not lost his eye for goal, by finishing as the club's top scorer for three consecutive seasons. He also appeared in League and FA Cup finals for Wednesday, losing out to Arsenal on both occasions.

BRIGHT

He then moved to Charlton Athletic where he was part of Alan Curbishley's side that clinched promotion to Division One in 1998 after a dramatic Play-Off Final penalty shoot-out victory over Sunderland at Wembley.

Bright retired from top-class football at the end of the 1998/99 season and currently enjoys his role as a club ambassador.

FULL NAME:
Mark Abraham Bright

POSITION:
Forward

DATE OF BIRTH:
6 February 1962

PLACE OF BIRTH:
Stoke-on-Trent

CRYSTAL PALACE DEBUT:
15 November 1986

APPEARANCES:
286

GOALS:
113

FULL NAME:
John Burridge

POSITION:
Goalkeeper

DATE OF BIRTH:
3 December 1951

PLACE OF BIRTH:
Great Clifton (Cumbria)

CRYSTAL PALACE DEBUT:
18 March 1978

APPEARANCES:
102

John 'Budgie' Burridge was a flamboyant and often extrovert goalkeeper, who played for no fewer than 29 clubs in a career spanning almost thirty years.

Born in the Cumbrian mining village of Great Clifton, Burridge began his career at nearby Workington at the age of 15 and after two seasons at Borough Park, he moved down the coast to join Blackpool. It was while at Bloomfield Road that Burridge won his first honour in the top-class game, picking up a winners medal after producing a Man of the Match performance, as the Seasiders defeated Bologna in the 1971 Anglo-Italian Cup Final.

He then moved on to Aston Villa and in March 1978, after a brief loan spell at Southend United, he was signed by Palace boss Terry Venables for a fee of £65,000. A real character, Budgie soon endeared himself to the Selhurst Park faithful with even his pre-match warm-up routine providing great entertainment for the Palace fans.

He made his debut in a 0-0 draw against Brighton a few days after signing, but the following season he was in outstanding form, conceding only 24 goals as Palace lifted the Second Division title. However, after only two-and-a-half seasons at Selhurst Park, he moved across London to rejoin Terry Venables, who had just taken over the Queens Park Rangers hot-seat.

BURRIDGE

Thereafter he played for a procession of clubs including Manchester City where, in the 1994/95 season, he became the oldest player to appear in the Premier League at the age of 43 years, 4 months and 26 days. Burridge still refused to hang up his gloves, playing on for another three years before finally calling it a day in 1997 after a brief spell as player-manager with non-league Blyth Spartans.

FULL NAME:
Daniel Paul Butterfield

POSITION:
Defender

DATE OF BIRTH:
21 November 1979

PLACE OF BIRTH:
Boston, Lincolnshire

CRYSTAL PALACE DEBUT:
10 August 2002

APPEARANCES:
269

GOALS:
10

Born in Boston, Danny Butterfield began his playing career with Grimsby Town, where he was used almost exclusively in the right-back role. The highlight of Danny's career at Blundell Park was undoubtedly the 1997/98 season, when he was part of the squad that lifted the FA Trophy and also clinched promotion to Division One via the Play-Offs.

In 2002, Butterfield turned down the opportunity of a new contract and moved to Selhurst Park where he soon became hugely popular with the Palace supporters. In his first two seasons at the club he was virtually ever-present and in 2004, he was a key player in the Palace side that won promotion to the Premier League, with a 1-0 Play-Off Final victory over West Ham United at the Millennium Stadium, Cardiff.

Injuries and the form of the emerging Emmerson Boyce, meant Butterfield's appearances in the top flight were limited and midway through the 2008/09 season he joined Charlton Athletic on loan. However, the following season he regained his place in the Palace side, initially in his accustomed right-back role and then as a makeshift striker, where amazingly, he set a club record by netting the fastest-ever hat-trick by a Palace player. Danny's three goals in the 3-1 victory over Wolves in a FA Cup Fourth Round replay, were scored in the space of only six minutes and 48 seconds and were described as 'the perfect hat-trick' - one with each foot and another with his head.

BUTTERFIELD

Butterfield's Palace career came to an end in July 2010 when he joined Southampton, but after initially doing well at the Dell, injuries began to limit his chances of first-team football. After three years with the Saints, Danny headed north to join Carlisle United and now plies his trade with Exeter City where he has recently signed a player/coach deal with the League Two side.

FULL NAME:
John Joseph Byrne

POSITION:
Forward

DATE OF BIRTH:
13 May 1939

PLACE OF BIRTH:
West Horsley, Surrey

CRYSTAL PALACE DEBUT:
First: 13 October 1956
Second: 25 February 1967

APPEARANCES:
259

GOALS:
101

Still a legend at Selhurst Park, Johnny Byrne is regarded by many as the finest goal-scorer ever to appear in a Palace shirt. Born in West Horsley, Surrey, he was first spotted by Vince Blore, a goalkeeper with Palace and West Ham in the pre-war era. Byrne signed for the Glaziers in May 1956, with the club at arguably the lowest ebb in its entire history, having been forced to apply for re-election after finishing 23rd in Division Three South.

Byrne made 14 appearances during the following campaign and whilst he continued to score regularly, Palace never really looked like serious promotion contenders. However, the 1960/61 season saw a massive upturn in the club's fortunes, not least through the goal-scoring exploits of their young centre-forward, who netted 30 goals to help them clinch promotion.

In a remarkable campaign, Byrne also became the first-ever player to be capped at U23 level while playing in the fourth tier of English football. Full international honours followed in November 1961 when he was selected to play against Northern Ireland at Wembley in the Home International Championships, although this was to be the only cap he won as a Palace player.

It was perhaps, inevitable that a player of Byrne's ability would eventually move up to the top flight and it came as no surprise when, in March 1962,

BYRNE

West Ham United paid a British record transfer fee of £65,000 for his services. At Upton Park he teamed up with the likes of Bobby Moore, Geoff Hurst and the up-and-coming Martin Peters, at the start of what was to be a halcyon period for the Hammers.

FULL NAME:
John Joseph Byrne

POSITION:
Forward

DATE OF BIRTH:
13 May 1939

PLACE OF BIRTH:
West Horsley, Surrey

CRYSTAL PALACE DEBUT:
First: 13 October 1956
Second: 25 February 1967

APPEARANCES:
259

GOALS:
101

In 1964, Byrne was part of the Hammers team that beat Preston North End to lift the FA Cup, which capped a tremendous season that saw him amass 33 goals in 45 games and also pick up the Hammer of the Year award.

A year later, the Irons were back at Wembley again, this time to lift the European Cup-Winners' Cup with a 2-0 victory over TSV Munich, although an injury sustained in the England-Scotland match a few weeks earlier, denied Byrne a place in the final.

On the international front, Byrne picked up a further ten caps during his time with the Hammers and was desperately unlucky to miss out on the 1962 and 1966 World Cup Finals. In fact, in 1962 it was strongly rumoured that he would have been selected for the tournament in Chile, but was overlooked by the England selectors after a confrontation with former England full-back Don Howe in a league game at the Hawthorns.

After five years at the Boleyn Ground, Byrne returned to Selhurst Park in a £45,000 deal, adding to his goal tally and taking his overall total for Palace to over 100, putting him fourth in the all-time scorers list. A year later he moved to Fulham and then out to South Africa where he played for Durban City, eventually becoming manager. Byrne continued to coach in South Africa until he died suddenly of a heart attack in Cape Town in October 1999, aged 60.

BYRNE

For those who saw him play, Johnny Byrne will be remembered as one of the finest and most talented players to have appeared for the club and by his colleagues as a great character in the dressing room, so much so that they nicknamed him 'Budgie' due to his constant chattering!

A stalwart central defender, Jim Cannon was an almost permanent fixture in the heart of the Palace defence for the best part of sixteen seasons, in the 1970s and 80s. Born in Glasgow, Cannon initially had trials with Manchester City, before being signed by Palace manager Bert Head as an apprentice in October 1970.

After winning Scottish Youth international honours, he was handed his debut by Malcolm Allison in a Division One fixture against Chelsea at Selhurst Park. Cannon's introduction to top-flight football could hardly have been more eventful as he was booked and then scored in a 2-0 win, Palace's only victory over another London side in a campaign that saw them relegated to Division Two.

The following campaign saw Palace slip into Division Three and Cannon's steadying influence at the back, proved vital as the club tried to arrest the slide. The Scot rarely missed a game and when they did clinch promotion in 1977, he was an ever-present in the side. A year later, he was voted Palace's Player of the Year.

In 1985, Cannon broke Terry Long's league appearance record for the club, eventually going on to make over 650 appearances for the Eagles and in April 1988 his magnificent service to the club was rewarded with a testimonial against Tottenham Hotspur.

CANNON

Cannon's love affair with the club ended in May 1988 when he was surprisingly released and then joined Croydon, after which he teamed up with former Palace colleague Peter Taylor, who was player-manager at Dartford. In 2005, Cannon was voted into Palace's Centenary XI, narrowly missing out to Ian Wright for the Player of the Century award.

FULL NAME:
James Anthony Cannon

POSITION:
Defender

DATE OF BIRTH:
2 October 1953

PLACE OF BIRTH:
Glasgow

CRYSTAL PALACE DEBUT:
31 March 1973

APPEARANCES:
660

GOALS:
35

Shaun Derry was a tough-tackling midfielder who enjoyed two spells at Crystal Palace during a playing career spanning thirteen seasons. Born in Nottingham, Derry joined local club Notts County straight from school, eventually going on to make 82 appearances for the Magpies before being transferred to Sheffield United.

After two years at Bramall Lane, he was sold to Portsmouth for a fee of £700,000, eventually being appointed captain by Pompey boss Graham Rix. It was the arrival of Harry Redknapp as manager, that brought Derry's Fratton Park career to a close and during the 2002 close season he was transferred to Palace for a fee reported to be in the region of £400,000.

The Selhurst Park faithful soon took to Derry's aggressive, all-action style, as he quickly established himself in a defensive midfield role in front of the Palace back four. In his second season at the club he made 44 appearances as the Eagles made it back to the top flight via the Play-Offs and in the semi-final second leg at Sunderland, he set up the last-ditch equaliser for Darren Powell, that took the tie to penalties. However, the following campaign saw Derry struggle to hold down a regular place in the side and in February 2005, after a brief loan spell at Nottingham Forest, he moved on to Leeds United.

His debut at Elland Road got Derry off to a great start, when he scored in a 2-1 victory over West Ham United. He went on to enjoy two great seasons in Yorkshire, before being ruled out through injury midway through 2006/07.

DERRY

Derry never figured for the club again and in November 2007, he returned to Palace on loan, eventually making the move permanent by signing a three-year contract following a £150,000 transfer.

In his second season back at Selhurst Park, the popular midfielder took over as club captain, a position he held until joining up with his old Palace manager Neil Warnock at Queens Park Rangers during the 2010 close-season. In 2014, after the best part of four years at Loftus Road, Derry joined Millwall on loan before returning to Notts County as player-manager.

FULL NAME:
Shaun Peter Derry

POSITION:
Midfielder

DATE OF BIRTH:
6 December 1977

PLACE OF BIRTH:
Nottingham

CRYSTAL PALACE DEBUT:
First: 10 August 2002
Second: 24 November 2007

APPEARANCES:
226

GOALS:
3

A tall, dominant central defender, Ian Evans first came to prominence with Queens Park Rangers, having joined the club as an apprentice straight from school. Evans signed professional forms in 1970 and was a member of the Rangers team that clinched promotion to Division One in 1973. He joined Palace the following year in a deal that saw the Eagles star-winger Don Rogers move to Loftus Road.

Soon becoming a towering figure in the heart of the Palace defence, Evans rarely missed a game and was an ever-present in the team that brought Second Division football back to Selhurst Park in 1977. Despite being born in Surrey, Evans qualified to play for Wales through his ancestry and after winning his first full international cap he immediately became known as Taff to his Selhurst Park colleagues. He won all of his 13 international caps while at Palace and was at the peak of his game when he suffered a double leg fracture, following a challenge with George Best in a home game against Fulham in October 1978.

Sadly, despite eventually regaining match fitness, Evans was unable to win back his place in the side and in December 1979 he joined Barnsley on loan, before eventually making the move permanent in a £80,000 deal. At Oakwell, he helped the Yorkshire club win promotion from Division Three before brief spells at Exeter City and Cambridge United brought his playing career to a close.

EVANS

He then returned to Palace in the summer of 1984 as assistant to new manager Steve Coppell, before trying his hand in management at Swansea City. Evans was part of Mick McCarthy's coaching team when he was manager of the Republic of Ireland and then followed his boss, when he returned to league football management with first Sunderland and then Wolverhampton Wanderers.

FULL NAME:
Ian Peter Evans

POSITION:
Defender

DATE OF BIRTH:
30 January 1952

PLACE OF BIRTH:
Egham

CRYSTAL PALACE DEBUT:
18 September 1974

APPEARANCES:
163

GOALS:
16

FULL NAME:
Douglas Alan Freedman

POSITION:
Forward

DATE OF BIRTH:
21 January 1974

PLACE OF BIRTH:
Glasgow

CRYSTAL PALACE DEBUT:
First: 9 September 1995
Second: 24 October 2000

APPEARANCES:
368

GOALS:
108

For the best part of thirteen years, Dougie Freedman was a name synonymous with Crystal Palace Football Club, a period during which he enjoyed two spells with the Eagles, making more than 360 appearances and scoring 108 goals. However, it was one goal in particular that made Dougie something of a cult figure with the Palace faithful, a dramatic strike scored at Stockport in the final game of 2000/01 season.

At the time, Palace were embroiled in a desperate struggle for survival at the foot of Division One and over 3,000 fans travelled up to Lancashire for the game. With only minutes remaining there was still no score, a result which would have seen the Eagles relegated, when Freedman burst into the box to net the winner and send the travelling Palace hordes behind the goal into ecstasy.

Born in Glasgow, Freedman began his career south of the border in 1992, when he joined Queens Park Rangers, but after two years at the club he was given a free transfer, having failed to break into the Rangers' first team. Freedman then joined Barnet, making his debut at the start of the 1994/95 season, at the age of 20. He quickly became established as a the club's main striker, netting 24 goals in his first campaign and after only one season at Underhill, Palace paid out £800,000 for his services.

Freedman continued to hit the target regularly in Palace colours, scoring 20 goals in his first season at the club including a hat-trick against Grimsby Town, netted in the space of eleven minutes!

FREEDMAN

The following campaign, 1996/97, saw Palace clinch promotion to the Premier League via the Play-Offs and whilst Freedman was less prolific with only eleven goals, he did score two vital and dramatic strikes, when he came off the bench in the dying minutes of the semi-final against Wolves.

However, Freedman's taste of the Premier League was limited to seven games, when he was allowed to join Wolverhampton Wanderers on loan, before eventually signing permanently for the Midlands club.

His time at Molinuex lasted less than a year however and whilst he had continued to score regularly, the emergence of a young Robbie Keane persuaded the club to sell him to Nottingham Forest for a reported fee of £900,000.

Freedman's time at the City Ground was largely disappointing and after Forest were relegated in his first season at the club and the expected promotion challenge in his second campaign never materialised, he made a sentimental return to Palace, following a £600,000 transfer in October 2000.

After that all-important goal at Stockport, Freedman hit a rich vein of form the following season, netting 21 goals in all competitions as well a winning his first full international cap for Scotland, to add to his haul of eight at Under-21 level. The game was a World Cup qualifier at Hampden against Latvia and Freedman scored the equaliser in a 2-1 victory, ironically, a header past his Palace teammate Aleksandrs Kolonko.

In the seasons that followed, Freedman was used in a variety of roles and it was only after the arrival Iain Dowie as manager midway through the 2003/04 season, that he managed to re-establish himself as the club's first choice striker. It was a campaign that saw a dramatic turnaround in Palace's fortunes with a great run in the second half of the season, that saw them clinch promotion to the Premier League via the Play-Offs.

Freedman's second stay at Palace lasted eight seasons, but after spells with Leeds United and Southend United, he returned to Selhurst Park again in March 2010, this time in a coaching capacity. After a spell as caretaker-boss, he was eventually offered the manager's post and faired reasonably well in his new role, guiding the club to safety in his first season and a mid-table finish the following

FREEDMAN

campaign which included a 2-1 victory over Manchester United at Old Trafford in the League Cup.

The 2012/13 season started brightly for Palace and it came as a huge surprise to supporters when Freedman decided to join Bolton Wanderers, a club twelve places below them in the league. Freedman was in charge at Wanderers for almost two seasons, before leaving in October 2014. He is currently manager of Nottingham Forest.

FULL NAME:
Douglas Alan Freedman

POSITION:
Forward

DATE OF BIRTH:
21 January 1974

PLACE OF BIRTH:
Glasgow

CRYSTAL PALACE DEBUT:
First: 9 September 1995
Second: 24 October 2000

APPEARANCES:
368

GOALS:
108

37

FULL NAME:
Dean Dwight Joshua Gordon

POSITION:
Defender

DATE OF BIRTH:
10 February 1973

PLACE OF BIRTH:
Thornton Heath

CRYSTAL PALACE DEBUT:
8 October 1991

APPEARANCES:
241

GOALS:
23

Born in Thornton Heath, Dean Gordon was a product of the Crystal Palace youth system, signing professional forms during the summer of 1991. Dean made his first-team debut that October, although it would be two years before he finally became established as the club's regular left-back and for the next five seasons he was virtually an ever-present in the side.

Gordon was a tough-tackling left-back who also possessed real pace and his attacking forays down the left-flank soon became the trademark of his game. He was also noted for his explosive shooting and during his time at Selhurst Park, netted over 20 goals, many of the spectacular variety.

In May 1994, Gordon's outstanding form earned him international recognition when he was selected to play for the England Under-21 team against Russia in the Toulon Tournament in Bandol and he went on to win a further twelve Under-21 caps for his country during his time with Palace.

Dean played 241 games for Palace before a big-money move saw him join Middlesbrough in the summer of 1998. In his first season at the Riverside he was an ever-present in the team, eventually going to make over 60 appearances for the Teesside club, before joining Coventry City in July 2002.

GORDON

Thereafter, Dean played for numerous clubs including Apoel FC in Nicosia and a spell in New Zealand playing for Auckland City and New Zealand Knights before retiring from the game in 2009.

Dean now lives in Sunderland and coaches youngsters in the Wearside area as well as being an active campaigner for the Show Racism the Red Card organisation.

Born in Lambeth, Andy Gray was a member of Palace's youth team in the early 1980s, although when he was not offered a professional contract, he moved into non-league football with, first Corinthian Casuals and then Dulwich Hamlet. Ironically, it was while playing for the Isthmian League side during the 1983/1984 season that Palace boss Steve Coppell spotted the young striker's potential and invited him to move back to Selhurst Park.

After completing a £2,000 transfer from the non-league side, Gray quickly adapted to the higher grade of football and made his first-team debut in a 2-2 draw with Shrewsbury early in the 1984/85 season. The following season saw him lead the Palace attack netting eleven goals, but following the emergence of strikers Ian Wright and Mark Bright, Gray moved back to a midfield role where he began to produce some of the best football of his career. After three years at Selhurst Park, his form began to attract the attention of a number of clubs and in November 1987 he moved to Aston Villa for a fee of £150,000.

Andy was at Villa Park for two seasons and after being capped by England at Under-21 level, he helped the Midlands side clinch promotion in 1988, before heading back to London to join Queens Park Rangers.

GRAY

His stay at Loftus Road lasted only a matter of months however and during the 1989 close season, after only eleven appearances for Rangers, he returned to Selhurst Park in a £500,000 deal.

FULL NAME:
Andrew Arthur Gray

POSITION:
Midfielder

DATE OF BIRTH:
22 February 1964

PLACE OF BIRTH:
Lambeth

CRYSTAL PALACE DEBUT:
First: 9 December 1984
Second: 19 August 1989

APPEARANCES:
242

GOALS:
51

FULL NAME:
Andrew Arthur Gray

POSITION:
Midfielder

DATE OF BIRTH:
22 February 1964

PLACE OF BIRTH:
Lambeth

CRYSTAL PALACE DEBUT:
First: 9 December 1984
Second: 19 August 1989

APPEARANCES:
242

GOALS:
51

The 1989/90 season turned out to be a great one for Palace, as First Division survival was secured well before the end of the season and a great run in the FA Cup saw them reach the final before eventually losing to Manchester United in a replay.

The semi-final victory over Liverpool at Villa Park remains one of the greatest games in Palace's history and for Gray, a place in Eagles folklore for all time. With only minutes remaining, Palace were 3-2 down and heading out of the competition, when he headed a dramatic equaliser to take the tie into extra-time where Alan Pardew netted the winner.

The following campaign saw Gray in brilliant form, as Palace achieved their highest-ever position in the league, finishing third behind Arsenal and Liverpool, as well as lifting the Zenith Data Systems Cup with a 4-1 victory over Everton. To round off a great campaign, Gray won his solitary full international cap when he played for England in the European Championship qualifier against Poland in Lech Poznan.

The 1991/92 season saw Palace's title challenge fade and at the end of the campaign, Gray joined Tottenham Hotspur for a fee reported to be in the region of £900,000. His time at White Hart Lane lasted only two seasons, during which he made only 33 appearances and after a brief loan spell at Swindon, he was sold to Spanish club CA Marbella.

GRAY

In 2005, Andy was voted into Palace's Centenary XI and a year later he took up his first managerial appointment as head coach of Sierra Leone.

FULL NAME:
Vincent Mark Hilaire

POSITION:
Forward

DATE OF BIRTH:
10 October 1959

PLACE OF BIRTH:
Forest Gate, London

CRYSTAL PALACE DEBUT:
2 March 1977

APPEARANCES:
293

GOALS:
36

A highly talented winger who loved playing to the gallery, Vince Hilaire was born in Forest Gate and came to Palace as a youngster after being spotted playing for East London Schools. After progressing through the ranks at Selhurst Park, he signed professional forms in October 1976 and was handed his first team debut a few months later, when he came off the bench in a 3-2 defeat at Lincoln City.

However, it was the following season, 1978/79, that Hilaire really came to prominence in a tremendous campaign that saw the Eagles win promotion to the top flight after lifting the Second Division title. Hilaire made 30 league appearances for Palace that season, one of a number of talented youngsters who had come through the ranks after lifting the FA Youth Cup in 1977 and retaining the trophy the following season. Under manager Terry Venables, they would help to establish what many Palace fans still refer to as the Team of the Eighties.

Never a prolific goal-scorer, Hilaire was very much a provider who would consistently delight the Palace faithful with his vast array of tricks, whilst still setting up goalscoring opportunities for his colleagues. Not surprisingly, his style of play attracted some severe retribution from certain opponents and throughout his career he was subjected to more than his fair share of rough treatment.

HILAIRE

Nevertheless, he rarely reacted to this sort of intimidation although on one occasion in a game against Spurs in September 1980, after being floored by a particularly vicious challenge, he leapt to his feet to push his opponent to the ground only to find it was the referee - needless to say he was sent off!

FULL NAME:
Vincent Mark Hilaire

POSITION:
Forward

DATE OF BIRTH:
10 October 1959

PLACE OF BIRTH:
Forest Gate, London

CRYSTAL PALACE DEBUT:
2 March 1977

APPEARANCES:
293

GOALS:
36

For seven seasons Hilaire was an established member of the Palace team that had promised great things, yet in the final analysis had failed to become the force in the English game that many had predicted. In all he made almost 300 appearances for the Eagles, scoring 36 goals and was voted the club's Player of the Year by supporters in 1979 and 1980.

During his time with Palace, Hilaire won international honours for England at Youth and Under-23 level, playing alongside the likes of Glenn Hoddle, Bryan Robson and Gary Birtles, although sadly, full international recognition eluded him. He also enjoyed a loan spell playing in the North American Soccer League with San Jose Earthquakes during the summer of 1982.

Hilaire finally severed his ties with the club in 1984, when he was transferred to Luton Town in exchange for Trevor Aylott plus a £100,000 fee, a transfer it was reported, which had been orchestrated to raise much-needed funds for the South London club.

His stay at Kenilworth Road was short and after only six league appearances, he joined Portsmouth, where he stayed for four years before making the move north to Leeds United. He then played briefly for Stoke City and Exeter City before retiring from the game at the end of the 1991/92 season.

HILAIRE

Hilaire then had a spell as joint-manager of Waterlooville with former Palace teammate Billy Gilbert and later worked as a matchday hospitality host at Portsmouth and also as a local radio pundit.

FULL NAME:
Paul Alexander Hinshelwood

POSITION:
Defender

DATE OF BIRTH:
14 August 1956

PLACE OF BIRTH:
Bristol

CRYSTAL PALACE DEBUT:
17 September 1973

APPEARANCES:
319

GOALS:
28

Football certainly ran in the blood of the Hinshelwood family, with father Wally playing for Reading and Bristol City during the late 50s and early 60s and brothers Paul and Martin, both carving out careers in the professional game.

The brothers, who were brought up in Croydon, were spotted by Palace manager Arthur Rowe, playing in the final of the London FA Schools Cup in 1969 and both were offered apprenticeships at Selhurst Park soon afterwards. Whilst injury would ultimately cut short Martin's hopes of a lengthy career in the game, Paul went on to become something of a legend with Palace fans.

Playing as a striker, he made his first-team debut in a 1-0 defeat at Blackpool early in 1973/74, but scored in a 3-3 draw with Cardiff City at Selhurst Park a few days later. His brother Martin had made his debut the season before and the pair appeared regularly together in the seasons that followed, both helping Palace to clinch two promotions in three seasons to make it back to the First Division in 1979. By then, Paul had moved back into the Palace defence, forming a formidable full-back partnership with Kenny Sansom and in September 1977 he won his first England Under-21 cap when he was selected for the European Championship qualifier against Norway at Brighton.

He did not miss a single game during the 1979/80 campaign that brought top-flight football back to Selhurst Park and whilst their stay in the First Division lasted only two seasons, Paul was voted Palace's Player of the Year for both.

HINSHELWOOD

An outstanding and consistent performer, Hinshelwood enjoyed a tremendous career with the Eagles, netting 28 goals in 319 appearances and in 2005 he was voted into Palace's Centenary XI. In 1983, he eventually called time on his Palace career to join Oxford United and after helping his new club clinch the Third Division title he returned to London to join Millwall.

He then enjoyed further success as a member of the Lions' team that won promotion to Division Two, before eventually ending his career at Colchester United.

Cliff Holton was a centre-forward in the old mould, a traditional target man who was big and strong, who had the ability to score goals regularly at every club he played for.

Holton was born in Oxford and began his career with local club Oxford City, before joining Arsenal at the age of 18 in 1947. He made his debut during the 1949/50 season and after picking up a loser's medal in the 1952 FA Cup final against Newcastle United, he became a key member of the Gunners' team that won the First Division title in 1952/53, netting 19 goals.

Holton remained a first-team regular for another three seasons, before leaving Highbury to join Watford, where he scored a club record of 48 goals in his first full season at the club. He repeated the feat at his next club, Northampton Town, by netting 36 goals in the 1961/62 season, becoming one of a rare breed of strikers to set the all-time goal-scoring record for a season, at two different clubs.

By the time Holton signed for Crystal Palace in December 1962, he was 33 and coming towards the twilight of his career, but he soon proved he had lost none of his ferocity of shot or sharpness in front of goal. After netting nine league goals in his first season at Selhurst Park, he was joint top-scorer the following term with 20 in 43 league games, in a memorable season that saw Palace clinch promotion to Division Two. Now a great favourite with the Palace faithful, Holton continued to find the target regularly and he finished top scorer again with eleven goals as Palace finished in a credible eleventh place in their first season back in Division Two.

HOLTON

Holton's relatively brief career at Selhurst Park came to an end in May 1965, when he returned to Watford and three years later, after subsequent spells at Charlton Athletic and Leyton Orient, injury forced him to quit the game. He decided against going into coaching or management and left football to take up a career in engineering. Sadly, Cliff died suddenly while on holiday in 1996, aged 67.

FULL NAME:
Clifford Charles Holton

POSITION:
Centre Forward

DATE OF BIRTH:
29 April 1929

PLACE OF BIRTH:
Oxford

CRYSTAL PALACE DEBUT:
26 December 1962

APPEARANCES:
112

GOALS:
49

Although he was only at the club for two seasons, David Hopkin's place in Crystal Palace folklore was guaranteed, when he netted a dramatic last-minute winner against Sheffield United in the 1997 Division One Play-Off final at Wembley. There were literally seconds remaining when Palace won a corner and when Simon Rodger's cross was headed clear to the edge of the box, Hopkin was waiting to curl an absolute peach of a shot into the top corner of the net, to send Palace fans wild with delight. Moments later, the final whistle blew and Palace were in the Premiership.

An accomplished midfielder, Hopkin was born in Greenock and began his career with Morton, before joining Chelsea in 1992. His first team opportunities at Stamford Bridge were limited however and two years after joining the club he was sold to Palace for £850,000. Hopkin soon became the engine room, in Palace's midfield, his never-say-die approach to the game making him hugely popular with the Selhurst Park fans.

In June 1997, Hopkin won his first full international cap for Scotland, when he played in a 3-2 friendly victory over Malta in Valletta. A week later, he picked up his second cap, following the 1-0 win over Belarus in a 1998 World Cup Qualifier in Minsk, although that was the last cap he won as a Palace player. Shortly after returning home, Hopkin was sold to Leeds United for £3.25 million. During his three years at Elland Road he won a further five caps for his country, before it became apparent that he was no longer part of manager David O'Leary's plans

HOPKIN

and he moved on to nearby Bradford City for a fee of around £2.5 million. His stay at Valley Parade was short-lived however and after only eleven appearances, he found himself heading south for a second spell with Palace.

David finally ended his playing career back at Morton and after hanging up his boots he went into coaching, eventually having a spell as assistant manager at Cappielow. In January 2015 he was appointed assistant head coach at Livingston.

FULL NAME:
David Hopkin

POSITION:
Midfielder

DATE OF BIRTH:
21 August 1970

PLACE OF BIRTH:
Greenock

CRYSTAL PALACE DEBUT:
First: 12 August 1995
Second: 17 March 2001

APPEARANCES:
127

GOALS:
33

FULL NAME:
Michael Eamonn Hughes

POSITION:
Midfielder

DATE OF BIRTH:
2 August 1971

PLACE OF BIRTH:
Larne, Northern Ireland

CRYSTAL PALACE DEBUT:
16 August 2003

APPEARANCES:
141

GOALS:
10

Born in Larne, Northern Ireland, Michael Hughes began his career with Carrick Rangers, but in 1988, after only 18 appearances for the Irish League club, he was spotted by Manchester City and immediately joined the ground staff at Maine Road.

Hughes won his first full international cap for Northern Ireland during his time with City, but his first team appearances at club level were limited and in August 1992 he moved to France to join RC Strasbourg for £450,000. Hughes was with the French club for four years, although during this period he had a lengthy loan spell with West Ham United before eventually making the move permanent. He joined the Hammers on a free transfer and in doing so became the first player to move clubs under the newly-introduced Bosman ruling.

In 1997 Hughes joined Wimbledon in a £1.6 million transfer and enjoyed the best part of five years with the club, but became embroiled in a registration dispute, following a loan move to Birmingham City. The saga rumbled on for over twelve months before agreement was reached and he was able to sever his ties with the club. In October 2003 he signed for Palace on a free transfer, who ironically, were sharing Selhurst Park with Wimbledon at the time.

His all-action displays in an attacking midfield role quickly established Hughes as a firm fans' favourite and in his first season at the club, he helped them clinch promotion to the Premiership with a Play-Off final victory over West Ham United at the Millennium Stadium. Hughes' great leadership qualities prompted manager Iain Dowie to hand him the team captaincy for the forthcoming Premiership season.

HUGHES

Although relegation followed after only one season back in the top flight, Hughes continued to be a key figure in the Palace side for another two seasons, before he was released at the end of the 2006/07 campaign. He then linked up with Iain Dowie at Coventry City, who had taken over as manager at the Ricoh, before joining Southern League side St Neots Town as player-coach.

Hughes' first taste of management came in 2013 when he returned to Northern Ireland to take charge at his old club Carrick Rangers. He then took a financial interest in the club, eventually becoming chief executive and majority shareholder.

FULL NAME:
John Keith Jackson

POSITION:
Goalkeeper

DATE OF BIRTH:
5 September 1942

PLACE OF BIRTH:
Hammersmith

CRYSTAL PALACE DEBUT:
25 August 1964

APPEARANCES:
388

Born in Hammersmith, John Jackson had already been capped by England at Youth level when he joined Palace from St Clement Danes School in March 1962. He was soon progressing through the ranks at Selhurst Park, eventually being installed as understudy to regular first team 'keeper Bill Glazier. When Glazier left the club in 1964, Jackson was handed his debut and for the best part of the ten seasons that followed, he was the last line of the Palace defence, eventually clocking up 388 appearances.

A great favourite with the Selhurst Park faithful who nicknamed him Stonewall, after the famous American Civil War General. He was an outstanding and consistent performer between the sticks and desperately unlucky not to achieve full international recognition, although he was selected to represent the Football League against the Scottish League in March 1971. Unusually for a goalkeeper, Jackson was rarely injured and did not miss a single game during the 1968/69 season, as well as missing only four games in the four subsequent campaigns.

Jackson's Selhurst Park career came to an end in 1973 following a disagreement with new manager Malcolm Allison. He joined Leyton Orient, where he stayed for six years, which included a loan spell in America with St Louis Stars and California Surf. In 1979 he signed for Millwall and later played for Ipswich Town and Hereford United.

JACKSON

John made only one appearance for Ipswich, although his outstanding performance in a top-of-the-table victory over Manchester United brought praise from Town boss Bobby Robson, "Jackson was brilliant - we would have paid him a year's salary to make those saves, but it would be worth it!"

In 1983, after almost 700 league appearances, Jackson retired from top-class football and since then he has held a number of jobs including working for a golf magazine, after which, for a time he was goalkeeping coach for Brighton & Hove Albion.

In the late 1990s, Carlisle United's Matt Jansen was one of the most talented young players in the lower leagues and after helping the Cumbrian side to promotion, and victory in the Football League Trophy Final at Wembley in 1997, he was soon on the radar of the majority of English football's top clubs.

When Manchester United expressed an interest, it seemed odds-on that Jansen would end up at Old Trafford, particularly after Sir Alex Ferguson showed him around the famous ground and outlined his plans for blooding him into United's star-studded line-up. Crystal Palace were also desperate to sign the youngster, but seemed to have little chance in the face of such high-profile competition, yet Jansen turned down United in favour of a move to Selhurst Park.

He was immediately thrown into Palace's fight for survival with only seven games of the 1997/98 season remaining. As the season drew to a close, Jansen netted three goals, including a truly brilliant strike against Aston Villa at Villa Park, but was unable to prevent Palace dropping down to Division One.

Jansen's stay at Selhurst Park lasted less than twelve months, before he made a £4.1 million move to Blackburn Rovers. Nevertheless, those fans who were fortunate enough to see him perform in a Palace shirt, will no doubt recall many great performances and stunning goals, particularly a brace in the 5-1 demolition of Norwich City to cap a brilliant all-round display.

JANSEN

Jansen's outstanding form continued with Rovers, but sadly, tragedy struck in the summer of 2002 when he almost lost his life in a motorcycle accident in Rome. Jansen's form was never quite the same again and after spells with Coventry City and Bolton, he moved into non-league football, first with Wrexham and then Leigh Genesis, before finishing his playing career with Chorley, eventually taking over as manager in July 2015.

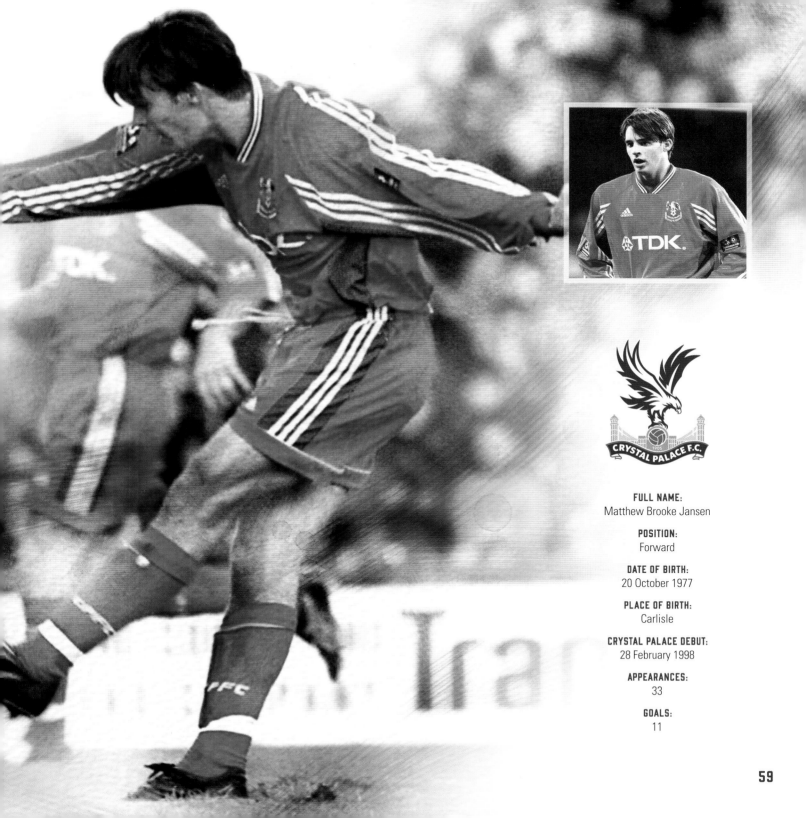

FULL NAME:
Matthew Brooke Jansen

POSITION:
Forward

DATE OF BIRTH:
20 October 1977

PLACE OF BIRTH:
Carlisle

CRYSTAL PALACE DEBUT:
28 February 1998

APPEARANCES:
33

GOALS:
11

FULL NAME:
Michael 'Mile' John Jedinak

POSITION:
Midfielder

DATE OF BIRTH:
3 August 1984

PLACE OF BIRTH:
Sydney, Australia

CRYSTAL PALACE DEBUT:
16 August 2011

APPEARANCES:
148

GOALS:
10

CORRECT AS OF 17 OCTOBER 2015

An outstanding defensive midfielder, Australian international Mile Jedinak began his playing career with Sydney United, before joining Turkish club Genclerbirligi SK in December 2008, after a spell with Central Coast Mariners. Jedinak spent the best part of three years with the Ankara-based outfit, before deciding to leave the club and a month later he arrived on the Premiership scene, signing for Crystal Palace.

The Selhurst Park faithful soon took to the powerfully built midfielder, who quickly settled into the holding midfield role, his high work-rate and ability in the tackle being a feature of his game. In the 2012/13 season, Jedinak was handed the captain's armband and after a superb campaign, he netted a dramatic last-minute winner against Peterborough United in the last game of the season to clinch a 3-2 victory and a place in the Play-Offs. He then captained the Eagles to victory in the final at Wembley where Kevin Phillips' extra-time penalty secured a 1-0 victory over Watford. To cap a truly wonderful season, Jedinak was voted Palace's Player of the Season.

Jedinak was in outstanding form throughout Palace's first season back in the top flight and opened his goalscoring account for the club when he netted from the spot in the 1-0 victory over West Ham United at Upton Park late in the season. However, it was a bittersweet moment for the Palace skipper, who chose not to celebrate as a mark of respect to Dylan Tombides, his fellow countryman who was being honoured at the match following his recent death through testicular cancer.

JEDINAK

Now virtually a permanent fixture in the Palace side, Jedinak played in every game of the 2013/14 season, missing only the final 30 minutes of the campaign, when he went off injured in the 2-2 draw with Fulham. The following term saw Jedinak pick up another award, when his stunning free-kick in the 3-1 victory over Liverpool at Selhurst Park was voted Palace's Goal of the Season.

Jedinak has also excelled on the international front and has picked up over 50 caps for his country. In 2015 he captained Australia to a major triumph, when they lifted the 2015 AFC Asian Cup with a 2-1 extra-time victory over South Korea in the final.

FULL NAME:
Andrew Johnson

POSITION:
Forward

DATE OF BIRTH:
10 February 1981

PLACE OF BIRTH:
Bedford

CRYSTAL PALACE DEBUT:
First: 10 August 2002
Second: 24 September 2014

APPEARANCES:
161

GOALS:
84

Andy Johnson was a product of Luton Town's youth academy, although his progress at Kenilworth Road was limited and his breakthrough into first-team football did not arrive until 1997, when he joined Birmingham City. At St Andrew's, Andy went on to make over 80 appearances for the Blues scoring 13 goals.

Not surprisingly, Johnson's move to Palace in 2002, caused little excitement among the Selhurst Park faithful, particularly as they were losing their star striker Clinton Morrison, who joined Birmingham City as part of a deal valued at £750,000. Nevertheless, it soon became apparent that the deal had been a real coup for the Eagles. Their new striker exploded onto the scene at Selhurst Park. Shortly after signing he netted a hat-trick against Brighton & Hove Albion and then repeated the feat in the very next game at Walsall.

However, in those early days, Johnson was often used in a wide role and it was only after the arrival of Iain Dowie as manager that he became Palace's regular front-man, forming a highly successful partnership with Neil Shipperley. In his second season at Selhurst Park he finished as the club's top scorer with 32 goals and the following campaign, 2003/04, he helped Palace stage a remarkable recovery to clinch promotion to the Premier League.

At the turn of the year, they were languishing in the lower reaches of Division One, yet an incredible run in the second half of the season saw them reach the Play-Offs and secure a 1-0 victory over West Ham in the final in Cardiff.

JOHNSON

FULL NAME:
Andrew Johnson

POSITION:
Forward

DATE OF BIRTH:
10 February 1981

PLACE OF BIRTH:
Bedford

CRYSTAL PALACE DEBUT:
First: 10 August 2002
Second: 24 September 2014

APPEARANCES:
161

GOALS:
84

Unfortunately, Palace were unable to sustain their progress and after only one season back in the top flight, they were relegated back to Division One. While Palace had struggled at the higher level, Johnson had continued to flourish, netting a commendable 21 goals, which at the time, was the highest-ever by a Palace player in a Premier League season.

His outstanding form in front of goal began to attract the attention of England boss Sven-Goran Eriksson and in February 2005 he won his first England cap, coming off the bench to replace Wayne Rooney against the Netherlands at Villa Park.

With Palace now back in English football's second tier, there was much speculation about Andy's future at the club, however, this was quickly quelled during the 2005 close-season when he committed himself to the club by signing a new five-year contract. The return of Clinton Morrison to Selhurst Park saw a new strike partner playing alongside Johnson and the club came close to promotion at the first time of asking, when they made it to the Play-Offs only to lose at the semi-final stage to Watford.

Again, Johnson was being linked with a number of Premier League clubs and it came as no surprise when Palace accepted an offer of £8.5 million from Everton for his services. He had enjoyed a tremendous career at Selhurst Park netting an impressive 84 goals in 161 appearances as well as being named Player of the Year in 2004 and also in 2005, the same year he was acknowledged as one of Palace's all-time greats, when he was named in the their Centenary XI.

JOHNSON

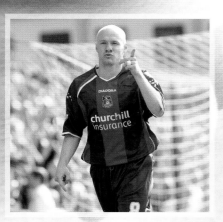

At Goodison Park, Johnson's career continued to flourish, while on the international stage he went on to win nine caps for his country. A move to Fulham followed in 2008 and after four seasons at Craven Cottage he joined Queens Park Rangers. In September 2014, Andy briefly returned to Palace in a coaching capacity and made a solitary appearance in the 3-2 League Cup defeat against Newcastle United at Selhurst Park.

FULL NAME:
Stephen Dennis Kember

POSITION:
Midfielder

DATE OF BIRTH:
8 December 1948

PLACE OF BIRTH:
Croydon

CRYSTAL PALACE DEBUT:
First: 1 January 1966
Second: 4 November 1978

APPEARANCES:
291

GOALS:
38

A supremely talented midfielder, Steve Kember was signed as a youngster by Palace manager Bert Head in July 1965 and signed professional forms on his 17th birthday. He was immediately drafted into the first-team squad and was handed his debut a few weeks later on New Year's Day 1966, in a Division Two clash against Bristol City at Ashton Gate.

Operating in a central midfield role, Kember's resourceful and creative play quickly established him as a real favourite with Palace fans and he soon became a fixture in a Palace side chasing promotion to Division One. The dream of top-flight football for the first time in the club's history was finally realised in 1969 and Kember claimed his place in Palace folklore when he netted the winning goal in the vital 3-2 victory over Fulham, in the final home game of the season.

He continued to shine in the top flight and won his first Under-23 cap for England in October 1970 when he played in a 3-1 victory over West Germany at Filbert Street. It was a great season for Kember, who was also appointed Palace captain, taking over from John Sewell, as he helped the Glaziers to safety after a desperate relegation battle.

In September 1971 manager Bert Head needed funds to overhaul the team after a poor start, so the club decided to cash in on their prized asset after accepting a club record bid of £170,000 from Chelsea. At Stamford Bridge Kember found himself playing alongside some of the most talented players in the English game, but in the years that followed, the club fell into decline eventually being relegated at the end of the 1974/75 season.

KEMBER

Steve then joined Leicester City and for his first two seasons with the Foxes, he was almost a permanent fixture in the side. Eventually, his appearances became less frequent and in October 1978, Terry Venables moved in to take the midfielder back to Palace in a £50,000 deal.

Kember brought vast experience to the young Palace side and in 1979 helped them clinch promotion back to Division One.

In 1980, he severed his playing ties with the club when he joined Vancouver Whitecaps before returning to Selhurst Park in a coaching capacity.

Kember enjoyed his first taste of management in November 1981, when he took over the Selhurst Park hot-seat from Dario Gradi and he enjoyed reasonable success too, by achieving Second Division survival and reaching the Sixth round of the FA Cup. However, during the 1982 close season, the Palace board took the surprise decision to appoint Alan Mullery as manager, a move not universally popular with the fans.

Kember then took charge of Isthmian League side Whyteleafe FC and guided them to promotion to Division One in 1990 as well as enjoying a decent run in the FA Cup. In 1993, he resumed his love affair with Palace, when he returned to Selhurst Park in a coaching capacity, a role he held until April 2001 when he was asked to take over as caretaker-manager after Alan Smith was dismissed, with the club on the verge of relegation. With only two games remaining and needing six points to survive, the odds were stacked against them, yet Kember inspired his team to two victories, the second of which was a last-gasp win at Stockport County.

Kember was then assistant to Steve Bruce and Trevor Francis, both short-term and unsuccessful managerial appointments, before taking over as manager again in his own right.

KEMBER

His first season, 2004/05, started brightly enough, but after only a few months, Palace's form dipped badly and when they found themselves in the relegation zone, manager and club parted ways. Kember is now a scout for the club.

FULL NAME:
Stephen Dennis Kember

POSITION:
Midfielder

DATE OF BIRTH:
8 December 1948

PLACE OF BIRTH:
Croydon

CRYSTAL PALACE DEBUT:
First: 1 January 1966
Second: 4 November 1978

APPEARANCES:
291

GOALS:
38

FULL NAME:
Attilio Lombardo

POSITION:
Midfielder

DATE OF BIRTH:
6 January 1966

PLACE OF BIRTH:
St. Maria la Fossa, Italy

CRYSTAL PALACE DEBUT:
9 August 1997

APPEARANCES:
48

GOALS:
10

Attilio Lombardo was already an established Italian international when he joined newly-promoted Crystal Palace, from Juventus, during the 1997 close-season. Having also won numerous major domestic honours during his time in Seria A, much was expected of the Italian wide-man and he wasted no time in delivering, when he scored on his debut in a 2-1 victory over Everton on the opening day of the 1997/98 season.

A pacey player with terrific acceleration and the ability to deliver accurate crosses, Attilio was soon receiving rave reviews for his exciting performances, which had inspired Palace to a promising start to their Premiership campaign. By November, they were sitting a comfortable tenth place and Attilio's sparkling form had earned him a recall to the Italian national squad. Unfortunately, an injury picked up while on international duty kept him out of the Palace side for some time and by the time he made his return to first-team duty, they had slipped to bottom spot.

At the same time there were major changes to the Selhurst Park management structure and after team boss Steve Coppell was appointed Director of Football, Lombardo was asked to take care of team affairs in a caretaker capacity alongside Tomas Brolin. Sadly, the pair were unable to turn the tide and after the inevitable relegation was confirmed they were relieved of their duties with three games left.

LOMBARDO

The appointment of Terry Venables as manager during the close-season raised hopes of a quick return to the Premiership, yet after a disappointing campaign Lombardo was sold to SS Lazio.

Although his stay at Selhurst Park was relatively short-lived, Lombardo will long be remembered as an exciting attacking player who thrilled the fans and it came as no surprise when they voted him into their Centenary XI.

BACK L-R: Barry Dyson, Jack Bannister, Bobby Woodruff, John Jackson, David Payne, Alan Stephenson and Bert Howe.
FRONT: Cliff Jackson, Brian Wood, Terry Long and Steve Kember.

A stalwart defender and one of Crystal Palace Football Club's greatest-ever servants, Terry Long was born in Tylers Green, Buckinghamshire and began his career as an amateur with Arsenal, before joining his local club Wycome Wanderers. Terry joined Crystal Palace in May 1955 and made his first-team debut in a 2-0 victory over Walsall at Selhurst Park early in the 1955/56 season.

In those early years, Palace were struggling in the lower reaches of Division Three South and Long became a key member of the team that brought about and upturn in the club's fortunes in the years ahead. Promotion was achieved in 1961, a season that saw Long achieve a milestone of 214 consecutive appearances for the club. A reliable and consistent defender, he remained a fixture in the side until promotion to Division One was achieved in 1969, but sadly, he was never given the opportunity to play in English football's top flight.

In all, Long made 480 appearances for Palace, surpassing the record set by Albert Harry in 1934 and his loyalty was rewarded in October 1966 with a benefit match against an All Stars XI. After his playing career ended, Long stayed on at Palace, working for manager Bert Head in a coaching capacity then assistant manager, a position he held until the arrival of Malcolm Allison as manager in 1973.

LONG

Long then joined his old Selhurst Park colleague George Petchey at Orient and then at Millwall where he was briefly appointed acting-manager after Petchey's departure in 1980.

FULL NAME:
Terence Anthony Long

POSITION:
Defender

DATE OF BIRTH:
17 November 1934

PLACE OF BIRTH:
Tylers Green, Buckinghamshire

CRYSTAL PALACE DEBUT:
28 September 1955

APPEARANCES:
480

GOALS:
18

FULL NAME:
Anthony Nigel Martyn

POSITION:
Goalkeeper

DATE OF BIRTH:
11 August 1966

PLACE OF BIRTH:
St Blazey, Cornwall

CRYSTAL PALACE DEBUT:
18 November 1989

APPEARANCES:
349

Crystal Palace certainly turned a few heads in November 1989, when they paid out £1 million to secure the services of Bristol Rovers young goalkeeper Nigel Martyn. At the time, the fee was a record for a goalkeeper and given the youngster's limited experience, it was seen by many as a huge gamble by manager Steve Coppell.

Newly-promoted Palace were leaking goals badly and a 9-0 hammering at Liverpool pretty much signalled the end of 'keeper Perry Suckling's career at Selhurst Park. Although lacking in top-flight experience, Martyn was quickly proving his worth and his arrival, together with the signing of central defender Andy Thorn from Newcastle United, immediately began to produce results and almost overnight Palace's season was transformed. A big imposing figure, yet remarkably agile, Martyn's presence inspired confidence in his defenders and helped Palace finish his first season at the club in 15th place, five points above the drop zone and come agonisingly close to lifting the FA Cup before eventually losing to Manchester United in a replay.

The following season, 1990/91, turned out to be anything but a fight for survival with Martyn in inspirational form between the sticks. Palace were in contention for the title, right up to the closing stages, before eventually finishing in third place, the highest-ever position in the club's history. In the way of consolation however, they lifted the Zenith Data Systems Cup with a 4-1 extra-time victory over Everton.

MARTYN

Martyn's outstanding form brought international recognition in 1992, when he was selected to play for England against the Commonwealth of Independent States in Moscow, but at Selhurst Park his team once again found themselves at the wrong end of the table, eventually being relegated on goal difference.

FULL NAME:
Anthony Nigel Martyn

POSITION:
Goalkeeper

DATE OF BIRTH:
11 August 1966

PLACE OF BIRTH:
St Blazey, Cornwall

CRYSTAL PALACE DEBUT:
18 November 1989

APPEARANCES:
349

Now one of the most sought after 'keepers in the English game, Martyn remained loyal to Palace, pledging his commitment to a sustained promotion challenge. His confidence was rewarded when they bounced back to the Premiership at the first attempt as First Division champions with 90 points.

Again, Palace struggled in the top league, but would have survived had the FA not decided to reduce the Premier League to twenty clubs, their fourth bottom finish consigning them back to Division One. Again there were questions surrounding Martyn's future at the club, particularly as a return to the lower level was appearing to affect his international career.

Nevertheless, even though there were rumours of a transfer request, he carried on in brilliant form, helping Palace reach the 1996 Division One Play-Offs only to lose in the final against Leicester City, to a Steve Claridge goal close to the end of extra-time. That defeat signalled the end of Martyn's career at Selhurst Park and in the summer of 1996, after 349 appearances for the Eagles, he joined high-flying Leeds United.

At Elland Road he got his first taste of European football at club level, producing some outstanding performances, in particular a Man of the Match display to deny AS Roma in the 1999/2000 UEFA Cup run. Martyn spent six years at the Yorkshire club, a period during which his international career flourished and even though he was very much an understudy to David Seaman for most of this period, he still ended up with an impressive 23 England caps.

MARTYN

In 2003, Martyn joined Everton, initially as cover for Richard Wright, but went on to make over 100 appearances in his three-year stay with the Toffees. His outstanding career finally came to an end when an ankle injury forced him to hang up his gloves at the end of the 2005/06 season.

FULL NAME:
John McCormick

POSITION:
Central Defender

DATE OF BIRTH:
18 July 1936

PLACE OF BIRTH:
Glasgow

CRYSTAL PALACE DEBUT:
27 August 1966

APPEARANCES:
225

GOALS:
7

Glasgow-born John McCormick began his career with local club Third Lanark, making his debut in 1959 and quickly establishing himself as the club's regular centre-half. McCormick spent five seasons at Cathkin Park and in the 1960/61 campaign, he helped the club to a commendable third-place finish in the Scottish First Division.

McCormick then joined Aberdeen, but his stay at Pittodrie was relatively brief and after making only 28 appearances he moved to England to join Palace during the1966 close-season. Signed for a fee of just £1,500, McCormick went on to enjoy eight wonderful seasons at Selhurst Park and was described by manager Bert Head as his greatest-ever signing.

After initially being used as an understudy to Alan Stephenson, McCormick soon became a fixture in the heart of the Palace defence and was an ever-present in the Palace side that clinched promotion to Division One for the first time in 1969. In the top flight, he came up against some of the top strikers in the English game, yet was totally unfazed by the higher level of football, consistently producing top-drawer performances alongside Mel Blyth, to help maintain his club's top-flight status.

A hugely popular player at the club, both with his colleagues and the supporters on the terraces, McCormick won Palace's first-ever Player of the Year award in 1972.

MCCORMICK

The following season he was awarded a testimonial in recognition of his loyalty to the club. He severed his ties with the Glaziers just after the start of the 1972/73 season and joined Wealdstone, helping the Southern League outfit lift the Division One title in his second season at the club.

After retiring from the game, McCormick returned to Scotland to run a hotel on the outskirts of Glasgow and currently lives in East Kilbride.

FULL NAME:
Clinton Hubert Morrison

POSITION:
Forward

DATE OF BIRTH:
14 May 1979

PLACE OF BIRTH:
Tooting

CRYSTAL PALACE DEBUT:
First: 10 May 1998
Second: 27 August 2005

APPEARANCES:
316

GOALS:
113

Born in Tooting, Clinton Morrison was an outstanding goalscorer during his two spells with Crystal Palace, enjoying a strike-rate of better than one goal in every three games. Right from the start, Morrison demonstrated his prowess in front of goal, scoring a dramatic injury-time winner on his debut against Sheffield Wednesday, in the final game of the 1997/98 season.

However, Morrison's taste of Premier League football was brief, as the club's relegation to Division One had been confirmed some weeks earlier. The arrival of Terry Venables during the close season raised hopes of a quick return to the top flight, but the campaign turned into one of huge disappointment both on and off the pitch. Morrison finished as the club's top scorer with 13 goals that helped secure a comfortable mid-table finish, but during the season Palace went into administration and at one point he agreed to play for the club without wages.

Morrison finished as the club's top scorer in the following two seasons and in August 2001, he won his first full international cap for the Republic of Ireland when he came off the bench to score his side's second goal in a 2-2 draw with Croatia. He was now regarded as one of the best strikers outside the top division and in 2002, Palace took the decision to cash in on their prized asset.

MORRISON

Morrison was sold to Premier League Birmingham City in a £4.25 million deal that also brought City striker Andy Johnson to Selhurst Park. Morrison spent three seasons at St Andrew's and although he continued to hit the target regularly, he never really settled at the Midlands club and in August 2005, he returned to Selhurst Park, ironically, forming a new striking partnership with Andy Johnson.

FULL NAME:
Clinton Hubert Morrison

POSITION:
Forward

DATE OF BIRTH:
14 May 1979

PLACE OF BIRTH:
Tooting

CRYSTAL PALACE DEBUT:
First: 10 May 1998
Second: 27 August 2005

APPEARANCES:
316

GOALS:
113

The 2007/08 season saw Morrison enter the Crystal Palace history books and pick up a Special Achievement Award when he became only the eighth player in the club's history to score a century of goals. The all-important goal came in a London derby against Queens Park Rangers, when he netted a dramatic equaliser in the 1-1 draw at Selhurst Park.

He then went on to score a further 13 goals in a campaign that saw Palace reach the Division One Play-Offs, with his final goal arriving in the 5-0 victory over Burnley, in the final game of the season. Sadly, it would be Morrison's last goal for the club and during the 2008 close-season he joined Coventry City, signing a two-year deal with the Sky Blues.

For most of his time with Palace, Morrison had worn his favourite number 10 shirt and when he was handed number 19 at the Ricoh Arena, he insisted on a plus-sign being inserted between the 1 and the 9, apparently, to signify 10. He stayed with the Sky Blues for two seasons, during which he was almost ever-present, playing over 90 games and scoring 21 goals, before being released at the end of the 2009/10 season.

Morrison then joined Sheffield Wednesday and got off to a great start when he scored on his debut, but following the arrival of manager Gary Megson, he found it increasingly difficult to hold down a regular place in the Owls' first team.

MORRISON

Morrison then had loan spells with MK Dons and Brentford, before being released by Wednesday at the end of the 2011/12 season. The next stop for the much-travelled striker was Colchester United, where he stayed for two years and then in November 2014, after briefly dropping into non-league football with Midland League side Long Eaton United, he signed for League Two club Exeter City.

FULL NAME:
Victor Moses

POSITION:
Forward

DATE OF BIRTH:
12 December 1990

PLACE OF BIRTH:
Lagos, Nigeria

CRYSTAL PALACE DEBUT:
6 November 2007

APPEARANCES:
69

GOALS:
11

Born in Lagos, Nigeria, Victor Moses arrived in Britain as an eleven-year-old and settled in London. He attended Stanley Technical High School in South Norwood, little more than a stone's throw away from Selhurst Park.

Moses' footballing talents were first spotted by Palace scouts when he was playing schools football and after he was invited to join the club's academy, his education continued at Whitgift School where he came under the guidance of former Arsenal and Chelsea star Colin Pates. A prolific goalscorer in schools football, Moses was quickly progressing through the ranks at Palace and in November 2007 made his first-team debut at the age of only 16.

A skilful winger with pace and the ability to find the target, Moses made 16 appearances during his first season in the team, helping Palace reach the Championship Play-Offs. At the end of the campaign he delighted Palace fans by signing a new contract, but in the seasons that followed, failure to secure a return to the Premier League began to take its toll on the club's finances.

Midway through the 2009/10 season Palace went into administration and Moses was sold to Wigan Athletic for £2.5 million. During his time at Selhurst Park he had developed into one of the most exciting young wingers in the English game and had been capped by England at U16, U17 and U19 levels.

MOSES

FULL NAME:
Victor Moses

POSITION:
Forward

DATE OF BIRTH:
12 December 1990

PLACE OF BIRTH:
Lagos, Nigeria

CRYSTAL PALACE DEBUT:
6 November 2007

APPEARANCES:
69

GOALS:
11

Victor spent two years with Wigan picking up his first England Under-21 cap before Chelsea tabled a bid for his signature at the start of the 2012/13 season. The transfer was prolonged with the Pensioners having to make no fewer than five bids before finally meeting Wigan's asking price.

Given the array of talent at Stamford Bridge, it was hardly surprising that Moses found it difficult to secure a regular place in the side in his first season at the club, although he did make a significant contribution to Chelsea's success in the Europa League. He scored four goals in six appearances during the tournament and was on the bench when they triumphed in the final with a 2-1 victory over Benfica in Amsterdam.

During the season, Moses was also called up by Nigeria for the 2013 Africa Cup of Nations and was in the team that lifted the trophy after a 1-0 victory over Burkina Faso in the final in Johannesburg.

At the start of the 2013/14 season, Moses joined Liverpool on loan and scored on his debut against Swansea City, however, the emergence of Raheem Sterling meant his first-team opportunities were limited and after a year at Anfield, he signed a loan deal with Stoke City. His time with the Potters was largely successful, although an injury towards the end of the season halted his progress.

MOSES

In September 2015, after returning to Stamford Bridge, Moses signed a four-year contract with Chelsea, but was soon on the move again, this time signing a season-long loan deal with West Ham United.

FULL NAME:
Peter Nicholas

POSITION:
Midfielder

DATE OF BIRTH:
10 November 1959

PLACE OF BIRTH:
Newport, Monmouth

CRYSTAL PALACE DEBUT:
First: 20 August 1977
Second: 22 October 1983

APPEARANCES:
199

GOALS:
16

Born in Newport, tough-tackling midfielder, Peter Nicholas joined Palace as a youngster and was a member of the club's highly successful and talented youth team that won the FA Youth Cup in 1977. Nicholas had signed professional forms in December 1976 and made his first team debut in a 3-0 victory over Millwall at the Den on the opening day of the 1977/78 season.

His all-action style, fearless tackling and unrelenting tenacity, made Nicholas an instant hit with Palace fans and he soon became established in the midfield destroyer role. In his second season in the first team, he was a key player in the Palace side that clinched promotion back to Division One and a few weeks after the end of the campaign, he won his first full international cap for Wales at the age of 19.

Having already been capped at Schoolboy, Youth and Under-21 levels, Nicholas' elevation to the top level arrived when he came off the bench during the closing stages of a 3-0 victory over Scotland in a Home International Championship match at Ninian Park. He went on to win 73 caps for his country.

Nicholas missed only three games during Palace's first season back in the top flight and was an outstanding performer throughout the campaign as they secured a credible 13th place in Division One.

NICHOLAS

However, the following season became something of a struggle with the club eventually finishing in bottom spot, but by then Nicholas had moved on to Arsenal in a £500,000 transfer.

Initially, Nicholas' time at Highbury was successful and he was virtually an ever-present in the side, but after a series of injuries during the 1982/83 season, he returned to Palace on loan. After a season back at Selhurst Park, the transfer was made permanent with Palace paying the Gunners £150,000 to secure Nicholas' return to the club.

By now, Peter was captain of the Welsh national team and continued to appear regularly for the Eagles, even though he rarely hit the heights of his previous time with the club. His second spell at Palace lasted two years. He then transferred to Luton Town, where he made over 100 appearances for the Hatters, before heading north of the border to join Aberdeen. In 1988 he returned to London to join Chelsea, where he picked up a Second Division championship medal, before finishing his playing career with Watford.

After retirement in 1993 Peter went into coaching, enjoying spells with Chelsea and Brentford, before returning to Palace for a third spell at the club, eventually being promoted to assistant manager. He then returned to Wales to take over as manager of Barry Town and guided the League of Wales side to the title in 2001. A spell in charge at Newport County followed and he was later manager of Llanelli when they won the Welsh Premier League title in 2008.

NICHOLAS

FULL NAME:
Peter Nicholas

POSITION:
Midfielder

DATE OF BIRTH:
10 November 1959

PLACE OF BIRTH:
Newport, Monmouth

CRYSTAL PALACE DEBUT:
First: 20 August 1977
Second: 22 October 1983

APPEARANCES:
199

GOALS:
16

FULL NAME:
Alan Scott Pardew

POSITION:
Midfielder

DATE OF BIRTH:
18 July 1961

PLACE OF BIRTH:
Wimbledon

CRYSTAL PALACE DEBUT:
11 November 1987

APPEARANCES:
168

GOALS:
12

Whatever Alan Pardew manages to achieve as Crystal Palace boss, it's highly unlikely he will ever eclipse the iconic moment of April 1990, when he headed home the dramatic extra-time winner against Liverpool to take the Eagles to Wembley.

The FA Cup semi-final at Villa Park was arguably the greatest and most dramatic game in Palace's entire history and is still talked about by fans to this day. The topsy-turvy tie had headed into extra-time with the score level at 3-3, when Palace won a corner on the left. When the ball was floated into the crowded penalty area, it was flicked on at the near post by Andy Thorn for Alan Pardew to appear, as if from nowhere, to head the ball home. It was an incredible moment and one which would guarantee Pardew a place in Palace folklore.

Pardew entered the top-level game relatively late in life and was approaching 26 years of age when Palace signed him from Yeovil Town for a modest fee of £7,500 in 1987. Having spent his early career entirely in non-league football, his signing could have been seen as something of a gamble, yet in the years ahead he was a consistent performer for the team. In his early days at Selhurst Park his efforts were not always appreciated by the fans on the terraces, but his colleagues had no doubt about his contribution to the team, particularly his battling qualities when the side was up against it.

Of course, Pardew's standing with the fans changed overnight on that incredible afternoon at Villa Park and ever since then he has enjoyed a cult status at the club.

PARDEW

He played in the both the final and the replay against Manchester United when Palace came desperately close to lifting the FA Cup and the following season he helped them achieve a third-place finish in the top flight.

Alan's career at Selhurst Park came to a close in November 1991, when he moved across London to join Charlton Athletic. In his first season with the Valiants, Pardew enjoyed an excellent campaign and only defeats in their final two games cost them a place in the Division Two Play-Offs.

He stayed with Charlton for four years and after a loan spell with Tottenham Hotspur, where he appeared in the 1995 UEFA Intertoto Cup, he moved on to join Barnet as player-coach.

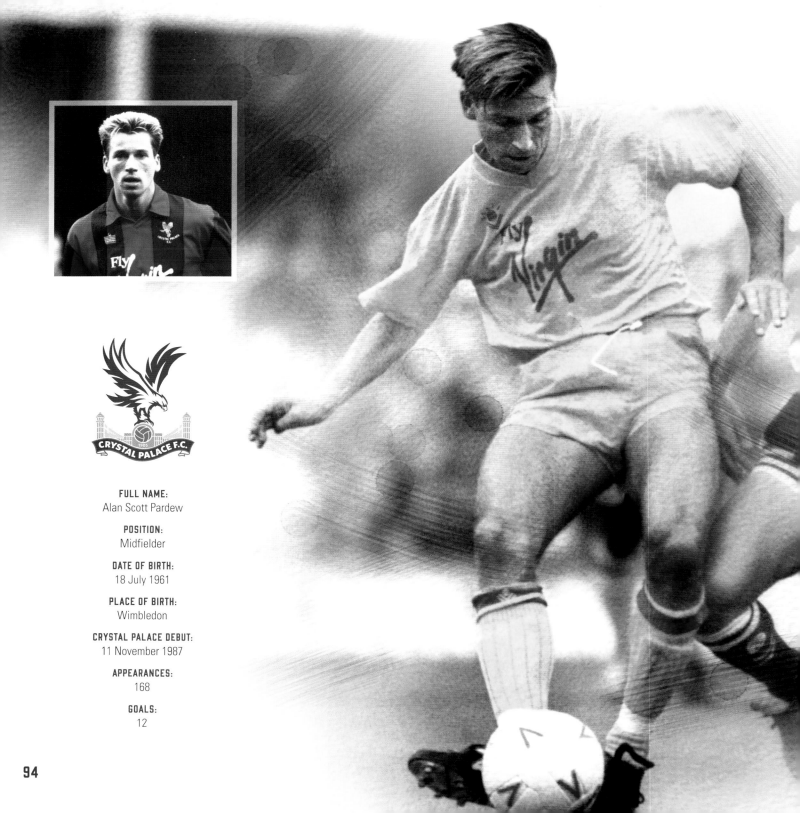

FULL NAME:
Alan Scott Pardew

POSITION:
Midfielder

DATE OF BIRTH:
18 July 1961

PLACE OF BIRTH:
Wimbledon

CRYSTAL PALACE DEBUT:
11 November 1987

APPEARANCES:
168

GOALS:
12

Pardew's first step on the managerial ladder came in 1997, when he followed his Barnet boss Terry Bullivant to Reading, taking on the post of reserve team manager. Two years later, after a spell as caretaker-manager, he was handed the post on a permanent basis and immediately inspired an upturn in the club's fortunes, eventually leading them to promotion to Division One.

Pardew's reputation as an up-and-coming young manager was becoming more widely known and it came as no surprise when he was offered the West Ham United job just after the start of the 2003/04 season. His stay in the Upton Park hot-seat lasted less than three years, although in his first season he took the Hammers to the Division One Play-Offs, only to lose to his former club, Crystal Palace, in the final. Then, in 2006, they came close to lifting the FA Cup, eventually losing out to Liverpool on penalties in the final. A poor run of form at the start of the following season brought an end to Pardew's reign at the Boleyn Ground.

His next managerial post was back at Charlton, where he signed a three-and-a-half-year contract, however, when he was unable to revive the club's ailing fortunes, he left by mutual consent after less than two years in the job. There then followed a relatively short spell in charge at Southampton, before he headed up to the North East to take over as manager of Newcastle United. During his time at St James' Park, Pardew guided the Magpies to a European place and won the Premier League Manager of the Year award in 2012.

PARDEW

Midway through the 2014/15 season, Pardew returned to his beloved Crystal Palace and masterminded a miraculous turnaround in the club's fortunes, taking them from relegation favourites to a comfortable mid-table position in the Premier League.

Born in Sydney, Australia to Croatian parents, Tony Popovic began his football career straight from school with Sydney United, where he progressed through the ranks to establish himself as a first-team regular. Popovic made over 160 appearances for United and was capped by Australia at every level during his time at the club before moving to Japan to join J League club Sanfecce Hiroshima in 1997. His stay with the Japanese outfit was highly successful and lasted until August 2001 when he signed for Palace on a free transfer.

Although Tony had had a pre-season trial with Palace a couple of years before, the fans knew little of the tall central defender when he first arrived at Selhurst Park, but his qualities soon became apparent to the Palace faithful, as he quickly established himself in the heart of the Eagles' defence. Having a great aerial presence, Popovic would often lend his weight to the attack, particularly on set-pieces and he opened his Palace account with two goals in the 5-0 demolition of Grimsby Town early in the 2001/02 season.

In Popovic's first two seasons at Selhurst Park, Palace failed to capitalise on early season promise and finished in mid-table in Division One, but in 2004, victory over West Ham United in the Play-Off final in Cardiff secured the coveted place in the Premier League. Popovic made 21 appearances in Palace's first season back in the top flight, but the campaign quickly turned into a battle for survival and ultimately relegation back to Division One.

POPOVIC

His career at Selhurst Park ended in June 2006 when he joined Al-Arabi Sports Club in Qatar. He then headed back to Australia to rejoin Sydney United before retiring from the game in November 2008 to bring to an end a 20-year career during which he picked up 58 full international caps for his country.

Tony had brief spell back at Palace in a coaching capacity before going into management and is currently coach of Australian A League side Western Sydney Wanderers.

FULL NAME:
Anthony Popovic

POSITION:
Central Defender

DATE OF BIRTH:
4 July 1973

PLACE OF BIRTH:
Sydney, Australia

CRYSTAL PALACE DEBUT:
21 August 2001

APPEARANCES:
144

GOALS:
8

FULL NAME:
Aki Riihilahti

POSITION:
Midfielder

DATE OF BIRTH:
9 September 1976

PLACE OF BIRTH:
Helsinki, Finland

CRYSTAL PALACE DEBUT:
31 March 2001

APPEARANCES:
178

GOALS:
14

Helsinki-born Aki Riihilahti began his career with HJK Helsinki, where he won just about every honour in Finnish domestic football, as well as helping his team qualify for the 1998/99 European Champions League. He also made his debut on the international stage against Cyprus in February 1998, the first of 69 caps he would go on to win for his country.

Riihilahti then moved to Norway to join Valerenga IF and then in 2001, after two seasons with the Oslo-based club, he joined Crystal Palace. A defensive midfielder, Riihilahti's style of play was built around work-rate, effort and commitment, which immediately endeared him to the Palace fans and he soon became something of a cult figure at Selhurst Park. His popularity was perhaps never better demonstrated than by the Finnish flag bearing the inscription 'AKI 15' which was hung from the stand behind one of the goals at Selhurst Park.

Riihilahti was a key figure in the Palace team that clinched promotion to the Premier League in 2004 and whilst relegation followed after only one season back in the top flight, he more than held his own against many of the best players in the English game. The following season saw his progress hampered by injuries and when his contract expired at the end of the 2005/06 season he moved to Germany to join FC Kaiserslautern.

RIIHILAHTI

He then enjoyed a spell with Swedish club Djurgardens IF, before returning home to re-join his first club, HJK Helsinki and in 2013, after various coaching roles, he was appointed Chief Executive Officer.

Riihilahti had enjoyed five tremendous seasons at Selhurst Park and still holds a place in the club's Hall of Fame for winning the most caps for his country while playing for Palace.

Born in Shoreham-by-Sea, Simon Rodger was a stalwart performer in the Crystal Palace midfield throughout the 1990s. Rodger joined Palace from non-league Bognor Regis Town in July 1990 and was quickly elevated to first-team football making his debut in 4-1 defeat at Sheffield Wednesday early in the 1991/92 season.

A versatile and combative midfielder, Rodger's whole-hearted approach to the game was quickly appreciated by the Palace supporters and during his twelve years at the club, he became a hugely popular figure on the Selhurst Park terraces.

During his time at the club, Palace experienced three promotions to the Premier League, but on each occasion success was quickly followed by relegation back to Division One. Whilst he did have loan spells with Manchester City and Stoke, Simon showed commendable loyalty to Palace throughout this period of instability and was rewarded in July 2002 with testimonial against Tottenham Hotspur at Selhurst Park. The fact that a crowd of over 13,000 turned up for the game was a clear indication of the huge popularity Rodger enjoyed with the Eagles supporters.

He had played well over 300 games for Palace when he was released by the club during the 2002 close-season and after a brief spell at non-league

RODGER

Woking he teamed up with his old boss Steve Coppell at Brighton & Hove Albion. Two years later, Rodger retired from football and currently lives on a farm in Surrey with his TV presenter wife, Alison Young.

FULL NAME:
Simon Lee Rodger

POSITION:
Midfielder

DATE OF BIRTH:
3 October 1971

PLACE OF BIRTH:
Shoreham-by-Sea, Sussex

CRYSTAL PALACE DEBUT:
5 October 1991

APPEARANCES:
328

GOALS:
12

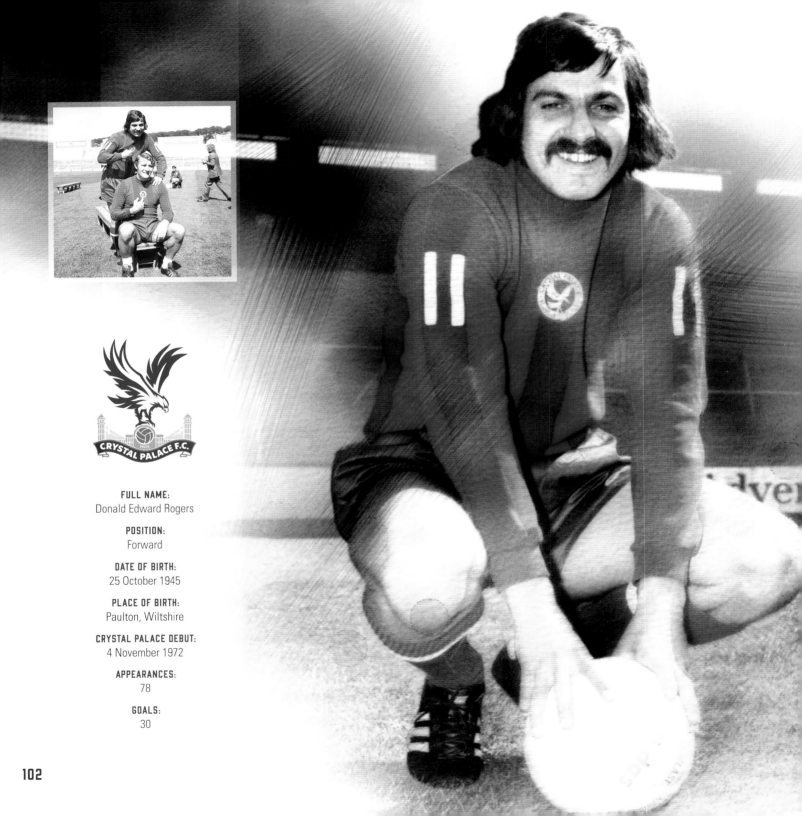

FULL NAME:
Donald Edward Rogers

POSITION:
Forward

DATE OF BIRTH:
25 October 1945

PLACE OF BIRTH:
Paulton, Wiltshire

CRYSTAL PALACE DEBUT:
4 November 1972

APPEARANCES:
78

GOALS:
30

A talented left-winger with the ability to score brilliant individual goals, Don Rogers spent just a little over two seasons with Palace, yet in that short time he established himself as something of a legend on the Selhurst Park terraces.

Born in Paulton, Wiltshire, Don began his career with Swindon Town, signing professional terms in October 1962. Once established in the Town first team, he soon earned a reputation as one of the best wingers outside of the top division and whilst several tempting offers of a move came his way, he continued to remain loyal to the Wiltshire club.

That loyalty was rewarded in 1969, when the Third Division side lifted the League Cup after a dramatic 3-1 victory over Arsenal at Wembley, with Rogers producing a match-winning performance, netting two of the goals. Rogers went on to make over 400 appearances for Swindon and was capped by England at Youth and Under-23 level and it seemed inevitable that he would eventually move into the top flight. In November 1972, it was his old boss Bert Head, now in charge at Selhurst Park, who persuaded Don to sever his ties with Swindon, Palace paying a reported £150,000 for his services.

Whilst Palace were relegated in his first season, he did produce some memorable moments, not least his two goals in the televised 5-0 demolition of Manchester United, one of which was a trademark solo effort, when he rounded Alex Stepney to roll the ball into the empty net.

ROGERS

Although not noted for his defensive abilities, as an attacking wide player, Rogers had few equals in the English game, and it came as a huge disappointment to many Palace fans when he was sold to Queens Park Rangers after just two seasons at the club. His time at Loftus Road was short lived however and after only 18 league appearances he returned to Swindon.

An exciting and creative player, John Salako spent eleven years at Crystal Palace after joining the club as a youngster in 1986. Born in Nigeria, Salako was a player with real pace and the ability to take on opposition defenders, which made him a firm fans' favourite at Selhurst Park. He was also a key member of the Palace team that reached the FA Cup final in 1990.

A year later, in June 1991, Salako won the first of his five international caps for England, when he came off the bench for the second half of a 1-0 victory over Australia in Sydney. However, his progress was halted when he sustained a serious knee injury against Leeds United in October 1991 which kept him out of action for the rest of the season. Returning at the start of the 1992/93 campaign, the knee again gave way in November which meant another operation and a long spell on the side-lines. Salako returned to the first team in September 1993 and on his first starting role, netted a stunning hat-trick against Stoke City. When the club was relegated from the Premiership again in May 1995, he brought his playing career at Selhurst Park to a close when he joined Coventry City.

Salako made over 270 appearances for Palace and whilst not particularly noted for his goal-scoring ability he did produce one or two brilliant strikes during his time with the club. In particular, Palace fans still talk about his goal against Nottingham Forest in an FA Cup-tie in 1991, when he caught Forest 'keeper Mark Crossley off his line with a terrific long-range effort from the edge of the centre circle.

SALAKO

Salako spent three years at Coventry before returning to London where he continued his career with Fulham, followed by spells with Charlton Athletic, Reading and Brentford. He retired from the game at the end of the 2004/05 season and worked as a matchday correspondent for Sky Sports.

In 2005, Salako was voted into Palace's Centenary XI and in August 2015 he renewed his association with the club, when he was appointed first-team coach.

FULL NAME:
John Akin Salako

POSITION:
Forward

DATE OF BIRTH:
11 February 1969

PLACE OF BIRTH:
Lagos, Nigeria

CRYSTAL PALACE DEBUT:
24 January 1987

APPEARANCES:
273

GOALS:
34

FULL NAME:
Kenneth Graham Sansom

POSITION:
Left Back

DATE OF BIRTH:
26 September 1958

PLACE OF BIRTH:
Camberwell

CRYSTAL PALACE DEBUT:
7 May 1975

APPEARANCES:
197

GOALS:
4

A full-back of outstanding ability, Kenny Sansom was signed in December 1975 while still at school and soon became established as captain of Palace's highly successful youth team that went on to lift the FA Youth Cup in consecutive seasons during the mid-70s.

Widely regarded as one of English football's brightest young prospects, he also skippered the England youth team, before making his first team debut for the Eagles at Tranmere Rovers on the final day of the 1974/75 season.

A pacey defender, strong in the tackle and a superb crosser of the ball, Sansom quickly became a permanent fixture in the Palace first-team, winning Player of the Year in his first season and enjoying a run of 156 consecutive appearances. He helped his side win promotion from Division Three in 1977 and the Second Division Championship two years later, picking up England Under-23 honours along the way and in May 1979, he made his debut at full international level in the goalless draw against Wales.

After a brilliant start to the 1979/80 season, Palace briefly topped the First Division and were being labelled by pundits as the Team of the Eighties. By now, Kenny was widely regarded as one of the finest full-backs in the English game and it came as no surprise when he was sold to Arsenal during the 1980 close-season.

SANSOM

The deal was reported to be in the region of £1 million and included another talented youngster, Clive Allen, who had only joined the Gunners a few weeks earlier and had yet to play in a competitive match.

Sansom quickly became a firm favourite at his new club and in 1981, was named Arsenal's Player of the Year after being an ever-present for two seasons. He also captained the Gunners to victory in the 1987 League Cup final at Wembley. After being a goal behind, Arsenal came back to triumph 2-1, with Sansom starting the move which led to Charlie Nicholas' late winner.

His career also blossomed on the international front and between 1980 and 1988 he rarely missed a game, playing in both the 1982 and 1986 World Cup Finals. In all, he made 86 appearances for England, a record at the time for a full-back, which was not overtaken until February 2011 by Ashley Cole, and Sansom's record 77 caps while playing for Arsenal, has only been bettered by Patrick Vieira.

Sansom's Highbury career came to an end in December 1988, when he made the move to the North East to join Newcastle United in a £300,000 deal. After only 20 appearances for the Magpies, he moved back to London to join Queens Park Rangers. Thereafter, he had spells Coventry City, Everton, Brentford and Watford, as well as venturing into non-league football with Croydon, Chertsey Town and Slough Town, before retiring from the game at the end of the 1994/95 season.

SANSOM

FULL NAME:
Kenneth Graham Sansom

POSITION:
Left Back

DATE OF BIRTH:
26 September 1958

PLACE OF BIRTH:
Camberwell

CRYSTAL PALACE DEBUT:
7 May 1975

APPEARANCES:
197

GOALS:
4

An outstanding and consistent defender, Brentford-born Richard Shaw was a product of Palace's youth system who went on to give great service during his nine years at Selhurst Park.

Something of a man-marking specialist, he is perhaps best remembered for his part in one of the most controversial incidents ever witnessed at Selhurst Park. The date was January 1995 and Shaw had been handed the task of marking Manchester United's flamboyant and temperamental French star, Eric Cantona, a task he stuck to rigidly throughout a torrid first half. Shortly after the break however, Cantona's patience broke and he kicked out violently at the Palace defender. The United star was promptly ordered off by referee Alan Wilkie, but the events that followed defied belief as the Frenchman suddenly dived into the crowd and launched a kung-fu-style kick at a Palace fan.

Although Palace were relegated that season, Richard enjoyed an outstanding campaign and was named Player of the Year, before being called up by England boss Terry Venables, as cover for the Umbro Cup squad.

Shaw was a key player for the Eagles throughout the late 80s and early 90s, helping them win two promotions, as well as picking up a Zenith Data Systems Cup winners medal and an FA Cup runners-up medal. He had made over 260 appearances for the club before his career at Selhurst Park finally came to a close in November 1995, when he was sold to Coventry City for £1 million.

SHAW

Shaw went on to enjoy a career spanning eleven years with the Sky Blues, picking up another Player of the Year award and finally being rewarded with a testimonial against Celtic in April 2006.

He finished his playing career with Millwall where he picked up his third Player of the Year award and is currently back at Selhurst Park where he is the Under-16s coach at the club's Academy.

FULL NAME:
Richard Edward Shaw

POSITION:
Defender

DATE OF BIRTH:
11 September 1968

PLACE OF BIRTH:
Brentford

CRYSTAL PALACE DEBUT:
19 September 1987

APPEARANCES:
268

GOALS:
3

FULL NAME:
Neil Jason Shipperley

POSITION:
Forward

DATE OF BIRTH:
30 October 1974

PLACE OF BIRTH:
Chatham

CRYSTAL PALACE DEBUT:
First: 26 October 1996
Second: 9 August 2003

APPEARANCES:
122

GOALS:
32

A powerfully-built striker who was capped by England at Under-21 level, Neil Shipperley first came to prominence with Chelsea and then Southampton, before joining Palace in a £1 million transfer from the Saints in October 1996.

Having spent four years in the Premier League, the move to Division One football was something of a step down for Shipperley, but one which proved to be relatively short as he helped his new club clinch promotion back to the top flight in his first season at Selhurst Park. Although relegation followed in the club's first season back in the Premier League, Shipperley continued to find the target and had netted 20 goals in 61 appearances before he was sold to Nottingham Forest in the summer of 1998.

His stay at the City Ground was relatively short and disappointing in terms of goal-scoring, but he rediscovered his touch at his next club, Barnsley, where he bagged 31 goals during his two-year stay at the Yorkshire club. Shipperley's next port of call was Wimbledon, who were playing their home fixtures at Selhurst Park at the time and when they eventually went into administration in 2003, he chose to sign for Palace for a second time.

Again, Shipperley helped the Eagles clinch promotion to the Premier League in 2004, by the way of the Play-Off final against West Ham United at the Millennium Stadium in Cardiff.

SHIPPERLEY

Not only did he captain the side, he also netted the only goal of the game, a typical striker's finish when he latched on to a loose ball to fire home, after Andy Johnson's shot had been parried by the Hammers 'keeper.

Shipperley's second spell at Selhurst Park lasted a little over two years and in 2005 he moved back up to Yorkshire, to join Sheffield United before finishing his top-class career with Brentford.

Shipperley then tried his hand in management with a number of non-league clubs, most recently with Southern League outfit Dunstable Town.

Simpson began his professional career with local Edinburgh club St Bernard's before moving south to non-league Kettering in 1927. He came to Palace's attention when the Northamptonshire club was drawn away to Palace in the FA Cup in November 1928. Although his club lost 2-0, some of the players so impressed Palace that Simpson was one of five signed, joining in the summer of 1929.

It was one of the shrewdest pieces of business ever by the club, as over the next six seasons, Simpson went on to become Palace's all-time record goalscorer, netting 165 goals from 195 League and Cup appearances. Although always appearing in the centre-forward position, Simpson had the skill and instinct to play across the line bringing his fellow forwards into play, especially his usual wingmen Albert Harry and George Clarke with whom he formed a formidable partnership. Simpson read the game brilliantly and could always find that split second of space to beat an opponent or lie deeper to receive the ball, proving that brains are sometimes better than brawn.

Simpson's debut came in September 1929 in a home game against Norwich City and he marked the occasion with a hat-trick, one of over fifteen he would claim in the next six years, while also scoring in the next four games. In that initial season, Simpson scored 36 league goals from just 34 games to set a club record for a season. The following campaign he was even better with 46 league goals and a further 8 in the FA Cup - club records that will surely never be broken. In October 1930, he scored six in succession in the 7-2 defeat of Exeter at Selhurst Park, a run of ten goals in three games for the centre-forward.

SIMPSON

Simpson was leading goalscorer in each of his first five seasons, but injuries began to take their toll, resulting in him being out of action for weeks at a time and in the summer of 1935, he moved across London to West Ham United and then to Reading.

When his football career ended Simpson took over a newsagent and tobacconist's shop near West Croydon. He passed away in March 1974, but his memory will never be forgotten at the club.

FULL NAME:
Peter Simpson

POSITION:
Forward

DATE OF BIRTH:
13 November 1904

PLACE OF BIRTH:
Leith, Edinburgh

CRYSTAL PALACE DEBUT:
14 September 1929

APPEARANCES:
195

GOALS:
165

FULL NAME:
Gareth Southgate

POSITION:
Defender/Midfielder

DATE OF BIRTH:
3 September 1970

PLACE OF BIRTH:
Watford

CRYSTAL PALACE DEBUT:
9 October 1990

APPEARANCES:
191

GOALS:
22

Born in Watford, Gareth Southgate was a product of the Crystal Palace youth system that produced so many good players during the late 1980s. Having already appeared in a couple of Cup games, he made his first team debut in a 3-0 defeat at Liverpool towards the end of the 1990/91 season, a result which effectively ended Palace's hopes of clinching the runners-up spot in Division One. Although he was employed as a centre-half that day, it was in a central midfield role that Southgate began to make a name for himself.

Although not particularly noted for his goal-scoring ability, his first strike for Palace was certainly a memorable one. It came on the opening day of the 1992/93 season against Blackburn Rovers at Selhurst Park, a brilliant looping volley from outside the box after a left-wing corner had been punched clear by Rovers 'keeper Bobby Mimms. Happiness turned to heartache, as Palace finished level on points with Oldham Athletic, but were relegated from the Premier League on goal difference.

During the 1993 close-season, following the departure of Geoff Thomas to Wolverhampton Wanderers, Southgate was installed as club captain and immediately inspired the Eagles to the Division One Championship. He also weighed in with a few goals, the most memorable of which was probably a superb solo effort in the 5-1 demolition of Portsmouth, when he ran half the length of the pitch to unleash a terrific shot into the Pompey net.

SOUTHGATE

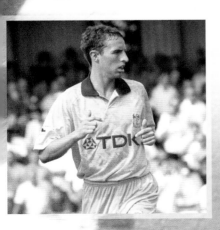

Having won promotion in something of a canter, Palace entered the 1994/95 season full of optimism, and although they finished fourth from bottom, they ended up being relegated due to the Premier League being reduced to 20 teams the following season.

The aftermath of relegation saw some of Palace's best players leave the club including Southgate, who was sold to Aston Villa in a deal reported to be in the region of £2.5 million.

Gareth played 191 games for Palace operating almost entirely in a central-midfield role, yet at Villa Park he was immediately moved back to the centre of the Aston Villa defence, an inspired decision by manager John Gregory that soon brought international recognition for his new signing.

Only a few months after joining the Midlands club, Gareth made his full international debut for England, coming off the bench in a 1-1 draw against Portugal at Wembley and then, to cap a great season, he was back at Wembley again, this time leading Villa to glory in the League Cup final with a 3-0 victory over Leeds United. During his time at Villa Park, Southgate's international career flourished and he represented England in the European Championships of 1996 and 2000 and also the France '98 World Cup finals.

Southgate went on to win 57 caps for his country, his final appearance coming in March 2004 in a 1-0 defeat against Sweden. By then, he had moved on to Middlesbrough, where he became the first captain to lift a major trophy for the Teesside club, when he led them to glory in the 2004 League Cup.

Soon afterwards however, a knee ligament injury brought his playing career to a close and in June 2006, he was appointed manager at the Riverside, a position he held for over three years. Southgate then had a spell in media work before being appointed as England Under-21 coach in August 2013.

SOUTHGATE

FULL NAME:
Gareth Southgate

POSITION:
Defender/Midfielder

DATE OF BIRTH:
3 September 1970

PLACE OF BIRTH:
Watford

CRYSTAL PALACE DEBUT:
9 October 1990

APPEARANCES:
191

GOALS:
22

Born in Buenos Aires, Argentina, Julian Speroni began his goalkeeping career with local team Club Atlético Platense, before moving to Scotland to join Scottish Premier League side Dundee. Speroni spent three highly successful seasons at Dens Park, but when the club hit financial difficulties in 2004, he was sold to Palace for £750,000.

Speroni played only a handful of games in his first season and for the best part of three years acted very much as understudy to the Hungarian international, Gabor Kiraly.

It was the 2007/08 season, before Julian finally established himself in the side, producing a series of outstanding performances to help his team reach the Division One Play-Offs. At the end of the season, he won Palace's Player of the Year award and proceeded to set a club record by retaining the honour in the following two campaigns. In 2013, Speroni helped Palace regain their place in the Premier League and in February 2015, he made his 347th League appearance for the club, breaking that record for a goalkeeper, previously set by another Palace legend John Jackson, who still holds the record for first team appearances at 388.

By now Speroni had long since been established as something of a cult hero with Palace fans, but at the end of the 2014/15 season, after picking up the Player of the Year award for a fourth time, it appeared his career at Selhurst Park might be at an end.

SPERONI

Both Sunderland and West Bromwich Albion were reportedly vying for his signature, but when Palace offered him a contract extension, the Argentinian 'keeper had no hesitation in pledging his immediate future to the club. In May 2015, Speroni's loyalty to the club was rewarded with a testimonial match against Dundee.

FULL NAME:
Julian Maria Speroni

POSITION:
Goalkeeper

DATE OF BIRTH:
18 May 1979

PLACE OF BIRTH:
Buenos Aires, Argentina

CRYSTAL PALACE DEBUT:
14 August 2004

APPEARANCES:
386

CORRECT AS OF 17 OCTOBER 2015

FULL NAME:
David Swindlehurst

POSITION:
Forward

DATE OF BIRTH:
6 January 1956

PLACE OF BIRTH:
Edgware

CRYSTAL PALACE DEBUT:
25 August 1973

APPEARANCES:
276

GOALS:
81

A tall, powerfully-built striker, Dave Swindlehurst came through the ranks at Selhurst Park and made his first-team debut in a 4-1 home defeat against Notts County, on the opening day of the 1973/74 season. However, it was the following season before the Edgware-born centre-forward became established as a first-team regular, when he finished the campaign with 14 goals in 34 league appearances.

In 1975/76, Palace enjoyed a great season by reaching the semi-finals of the FA Cup and although they were beaten by Southampton they had produced some terrific performances along the way. Swindlehurst was on target in the 1-1 draw against Millwall in the second round and netted the only goal of the game in a tremendous 1-0 victory over First Division giants Leeds United at Elland Road to take Palace into the fifth round. To cap a great season for the Palace striker, international recognition arrived when he was picked to play for England against Wales in an Under-21 international at Molineux.

For the next three seasons, Swindlehurst was a consistent goalscorer for Palace and topped the charts in the 1978/79 campaign, when he also netted arguably his most memorable goal for the club. It came in the last game of the season against Burnley at Selhurst Park, an encounter that Palace needed to win to clinch the Second Division title.

SWINDLEHURST

It was a night of high drama in front of a crowd of over 51,000 and Swindlehurst netted the second goal in a 2-0 victory, a terrific right-foot shot from outside the box to clinch the match and spark wild celebrations on the terraces.

FULL NAME:
David Swindlehurst

POSITION:
Forward

DATE OF BIRTH:
6 January 1956

PLACE OF BIRTH:
Edgware

CRYSTAL PALACE DEBUT:
25 August 1973

APPEARANCES:
276

GOALS:
81

Swindlehurst continued to find the target regularly in the top flight, helping Palace to a comfortable mid-table finish, however in April 1980, he was sold to Derby County for £400,000 to bring an end to his Selhurst Park career that saw him score an impressive 81 goals in 276 appearances.

Swindlehurst spent three seasons at the Baseball Ground, netting 33 goals in 125 appearances for the Rams, before returning to London to join West Ham United. In 1985, he became one of Lawrie McMenemy's first signings when the former Southampton boss took over as manager of Sunderland, an ill-fated period for the Wearside club, that eventually ended in relegation to Division Three. By then however, Swindlehurst had moved on, this time to try his luck abroad with Anorthosis Famagusta FC. His stay with the Cypriot club was brief and after only a few months, he returned to England to join Wimbledon. He then moved on to Colchester and in 1989, after a brief loan spell with Peterborough United, he finally retired from the top-class game.

Swindlehurst then moved into non-league football with Isthmian League clubs Bromley and Molesey, operating both as a player and a coach, before returning to Selhurst Park to join the coaching team in the club's youth academy. In 2001, he was promoted to reserve team manager, a post he held for 12 months.

SWINDLEHURST

FULL NAME:
Peter John Taylor

POSITION:
Forward

DATE OF BIRTH:
3 January 1953

PLACE OF BIRTH:
Rochford, Essex

CRYSTAL PALACE DEBUT:
13 October 1973

APPEARANCES:
142

GOALS:
39

An outstanding winger in the traditional mould, Peter Taylor had trials with Palace as a youngster, but eventually began his career with his local club Southend United. He was soon established in the first team at Roots Hall and was a key player when they clinched promotion to Division Three in 1972. Not surprisingly, the young winger's performances began to attract the attention of a number of top flight clubs and in October 1973, Palace boss Malcolm Allison persuaded Peter to join the Eagles in a £110,000 transfer.

At Selhurst Park his career blossomed and whilst Palace were relegated in his first season at the club, Taylor was named Player of the Year. He lifted the same honour in 1976 after arguably his best-ever season for the Eagles, when they narrowly missed promotion and reached the FA Cup semi-finals. In the cup in particular, Taylor was in inspirational form, netting two goals in a 3-2 victory over Chelsea in the fifth round at Stamford Bridge and then setting up the only goal of the game for Alan Whittle, in the quarter-final tie against Sunderland at Roker Park.

Soon afterwards, Taylor joined a rare breed of players to have been capped at full international level whilst playing in the third tier of English Football. His debut for England saw him score in a 2-1 victory over Wales at Wrexham, the first of the four caps he won while at Palace.

TAYLOR

Inevitably a step up to the First Division beckoned and in September 1976, he completed a move to Tottenham Hotspur for a record fee of £400,000. In all Peter made 142 appearances for Palace netting 39 goals, during four brilliant seasons, when he consistently delighted the Selhurst Park faithful with his direct, and often devastating style of wing play.

He went on to spend four years at White Hart Lane, where he experienced both the heartbreak of relegation and the joy of promotion before joining Orient in November 1980. In the latter part of Taylor's playing career he was much-travelled, enjoying spells with Oldham Athletic, Maidstone United, Exeter City, Chelmsford and Dartford, where he took his first steps into management in 1986.

Thereafter, he managed numerous clubs, soon becoming established as a highly regarded coach and in November 2000, while managing Leicester City, he was invited to take charge of the England team in a caretaker capacity for the international against Italy in Turin. Taylor also had two spells managing the national Under-21 side, together with a sentimental return to Selhurst Park to take over the managerial hot-seat in June 2006. Sadly, his second spell at the club did not end well and after 14 months in the job, parted ways with the club languishing perilously close to the bottom of the table.

TAYLOR

Taylor is still very much involved in the game and in May 2015, he was appointed head coach of Kerala Blasters in the Indian Super League.

FULL NAME:
Peter John Taylor

POSITION:
Forward

DATE OF BIRTH:
3 January 1953

PLACE OF BIRTH:
Rochford, Essex

CRYSTAL PALACE DEBUT:
13 October 1973

APPEARANCES:
142

GOALS:
39

FULL NAME:
Geoffrey Robert Thomas

POSITION:
Midfielder

DATE OF BIRTH:
5 August 1964

PLACE OF BIRTH:
Manchester

CRYSTAL PALACE DEBUT:
15 August 1987

APPEARANCES:
249

GOALS:
35

Geoff Thomas began his career playing non-league football while working as an electrician and was forced to take a pay-cut when the opportunity to join Rochdale arose in 1982. However, his progress at Spotland was slow and it was only after a move to Crewe Alexandra two years later, that his full potential began to be realised.

At Gresty Road, Thomas came under the guidance of Dario Gradi, a man with a huge reputation for developing young players and after scoring on his debut, he soon became a great favourite with the Crewe supporters. Playing predominantly in the centre of midfield, Thomas' performances began to attract the attention of a number of top clubs and in June 1987, Palace manager Steve Coppell secured his signature for a £50,000 fee.

It soon became apparent that the money had been well spent, with the new signing making an immediate impact at Selhurst Park and being named Player of the Season in his first campaign at the club. The following season, Thomas helped Palace clinch promotion back to the top flight and a year later he captained the Eagles in the FA Cup final against Manchester United at Wembley, before eventually losing 1-0 in the replay, after a dramatic 3-3 draw in the first game.

THOMAS

Perhaps the highlight of Geoff's time with Palace came in the 1990/91 season, when they finished third in the old First Division, the highest in the club's entire history. Thomas had been in outstanding form in the middle of the park and again picked up the supporters' Player of the Year award. Then in May 1991, to crown what had been a truly magnificent campaign, he won his first full international cap for England when he was selected to play in the European Championship Qualifier against Turkey in Izmir.

In all, Thomas won nine caps during his time at Selhurst Park, where he had established himself as one of the finest midfield players in the club's history. He finally left Palace in June 1993, moving north to join Wolverhampton Wanderers in an £800,000 deal, although his career at Molineux was blighted with injury and in his four seasons at the club, he made just 54 appearances. Thomas then moved to Nottingham Forest and had brief spells with Barnsley and Notts County before returning to Crewe Alexandra. Still hampered by injuries, his career came to an end in 2002, when he bowed out with a goal in an FA Cup-tie against Rotherham United.

Whilst Thomas had faced his fair share of challenges during his playing career, none came near to the one he encountered just a year after retiring when he was diagnosed with chronic myeloid leukaemia.

THOMAS

Thankfully, he went on to make a full recovery and since then, has worked tirelessly to raise funds for Leukaemia Research. In 2005, he won the BBC Sports Personality of the Year Helen Rollason Award after completing all 21 stages of the Tour de France and raising over £150,000 for the charity.

FULL NAME:
Geoffrey Robert Thomas

POSITION:
Midfielder

DATE OF BIRTH:
5 August 1964

PLACE OF BIRTH:
Manchester

CRYSTAL PALACE DEBUT:
15 August 1987

APPEARANCES:
249

GOALS:
35

133

FULL NAME:
Andrew Charles Thorn

POSITION:
Central Defender

DATE OF BIRTH:
12 November 1966

PLACE OF BIRTH:
Carshalton

CRYSTAL PALACE DEBUT:
9 December 1989

APPEARANCES:
168

GOALS:
7

A tough, uncompromising central defender, Andy Thorn began his career with Wimbledon, where he picked up five Under-21 caps for England and was part of the 'Crazy Gang' side that defied the odds, to lift the FA Cup with a 1-0 victory over Liverpool at Wembley in 1988.

The cup-winning team was broken up soon afterwards however, and Thorn was one of a number of players who moved on to pastures new, heading to the North East to join Newcastle United. His stay on Tyneside was brief and in November 1989, after only 36 appearances for the Magpies, Thorn returned to the capital and signed for Palace in a £650,000 deal.

He quickly became a firm favourite at Selhurst Park, his solid and consistent defensive displays alongside former Wimbledon colleague Eric Young, helping Palace preserve their Premiership status in the years that followed. Thorn was also in the Palace side that reached the FA Cup final in 1990 when they narrowly missed out on lifting the coveted trophy, losing to Manchester United in a replay and in his five years at the club he established a reputation as one the finest defenders in the English game.

Thorn's career at Palace came to an end in 1994 when he returned to Wimbledon and after spells with Hearts and Tranmere Rovers he hung up his boots to move into coaching.

THORN

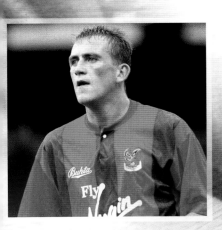

His first managerial post arrived in 2011, when he took over at Coventry City, but after only one season in charge at the Ricoh, he lost his job after being unable to save the club from relegation. Thorn later had a spell in charge at Kidderminster Harriers.

Arguably the finest goalscorer ever to wear a Palace shirt, Ian Wright was somewhat surprisingly overlooked by a number of clubs when he was in his teens and was approaching his 22nd birthday when he was signed from Greenwich Borough, by Palace boss Steve Coppell. Ian made his Eagles debut when he came off the bench in a 3-2 defeat against Huddersfield Town early in the 1985/86 season and finished the campaign as the club's second highest scorer with nine goals.

The following season saw Wright team up with Mark Bright, to form what would develop into one of the most devastating strike partnerships in the league and their goals were largely responsible in securing Palace's promotion to the top flight in 1989.

Crystal Palace had finished the campaign in third place and looked to have missed out when they trailed 3-1 to Blackburn Rovers after the first leg of the Play-Off final at Ewood Park, however, on a June afternoon of high drama at Selhurst Park, they managed to overturn the deficit with Wright netting twice in a famous 3-0 victory.

Their first season back in the top flight saw Palace finish in a credible 15th place and also marked Wright's arrival on the international scene, when he won his first England B cap in a 2-1 victory over Yugoslavia at the Den.

WRIGHT

Unfortunately his campaign was blighted by injury when he twice fractured a shin bone, although his return to action could hardly have been more dramatic. In his absence, Palace had reached the FA Cup final where they faced the might of Manchester United and manager Steve Coppell made what turned out to be an inspired decision when he selected Wright as one the substitutes.

FULL NAME:
Ian Edward Wright

POSITION:
Forward

DATE OF BIRTH:
3 November 1963

PLACE OF BIRTH:
Woolwich

CRYSTAL PALACE DEBUT:
31 August 1985

APPEARANCES:
277

GOALS:
117

FULL NAME:
Ian Edward Wright

POSITION:
Forward

DATE OF BIRTH:
3 November 1963

PLACE OF BIRTH:
Woolwich

CRYSTAL PALACE DEBUT:
31 August 1985

APPEARANCES:
277

GOALS:
117

With Palace trailing 2-1 with only 20 minutes remaining, Coppell took the decision to throw his star-striker into the fray and the results that followed could hardly have been more dramatic. Within three minutes Wright had netted the equaliser and when he put his side in front in extra-time the FA Cup seemed to be within touching distance, only for Mark Hughes to level for United and take the final to a replay. Sadly for Palace, it was very much a case of so near, yet so far, as a solitary Lee Martin goal won the replay for the Red Devils.

The following season saw Palace produce their best ever placing in English football's top division when they finished third and they also lifted the Zenith Data Systems Cup, with Wright scoring twice in a 4-1 victory over Everton in the final. A wonderful campaign saw the Eagles' star-striker score his 100th goal for the club and also win the first of his 39 full international caps for England, when he played in a 2-0 victory over Cameroon at Wembley.

Wright's Selhurst Park career came to a close in September 1991, when he joined Arsenal in a £2.5 million deal. During his time with Palace he netted an impressive 117 goals in 277 appearances and in 2005 he received the ultimate accolade when he was named Player of the Century by the club's supporters.

WRIGHT

Wright remains a true legend at Selhurst Park and also enjoys similar status at Highbury, where he won just about every major domestic honour. He spent seven seasons with the Gunners, before moving on to West Ham United and later spells with Nottingham Forest, Celtic and Burnley before retiring from the game at the end of the 1999/2000 season.

Soon afterwards Ian was awarded an MBE in recognition of his services to football, before taking up a career in media work, where he regularly provides expert analysis on the game's club and international scene.

FULL NAME:
Eric Young

POSITION:
Central Defender

DATE OF BIRTH:
25 March 1960

PLACE OF BIRTH:
Singapore

CRYSTAL PALACE DEBUT:
25 August 1990

APPEARANCES:
204

GOALS:
17

Nicknamed Ninja, due to his trademark headband, Singapore-born Eric Young was a tall, commanding central-defender who first came to prominence in league football with Brighton & Hove Albion, after making his debut on the opening day of the 1982/83 season.

Young spent five seasons at the Goldstone Ground, before joining Wimbledon during the 1987 close season for a fee of £70,000 and in his first campaign he was a key performer in the 'Crazy Gang' team that lifted the FA Cup, after a dramatic 1-0 victory over Liverpool in the final at Wembley. In May 1990, at the age of 30, Young made his debut on the international stage, playing for Wales in a friendly international against Costa Rica at Ninian Park, the first of 21 caps he won for his country.

Young spent three years with the Dons, before joining Palace in a £850,000 move during the 1990 close-season where he teamed up with his former Wimbledon defensive partner, Andy Thorn, who had moved to Selhurst Park twelve months earlier. At Plough Lane the pair had developed into one of the best defensive partnerships in the top flight and their great form continued with Palace, where Eric produced arguably the best form of his career, helping his new club to a third place finish in his first season.

YOUNG

A consistent performer and a great favourite with the fans, Young was an outstanding figure in the heart of Palace's defence for the best part of five seasons, before he joined Wolverhampton Wanderers the end of the 1994/95 campaign.

He enjoyed two seasons with the Midlands club and after bringing his top-class career to a close, Young moved into non-league football before finally retiring from the game at the age of 41.

FULL NAME:
Dazet Wilfried Armel Zaha

POSITION:
Forward

DATE OF BIRTH:
10 November 1992

PLACE OF BIRTH:
Ivory Coast

CRYSTAL PALACE DEBUT:
First: 27 March 2010
Second: 30 August 2014

APPEARANCES:
189

GOALS:
24

CORRECT AS OF 17 OCTOBER 2015

An immensely talented winger, **Wilfried Zaha** was born on the Ivory Coast, but after moving to England with his family, he spent his formative years living in Thornton Heath and joined the Crystal Palace Academy at the age of 12. Zaha's progress to first-team football was rapid and he made his debut at the age of only 17, when coming off the bench in the closing stages of a Championship match against Cardiff City at Selhurst Park on 27 March 2010.

During the 2010 close season, Zaha committed his future to the club by signing a two-year contract and the following season saw him make 44 appearances, his skilful and exciting wing play bringing countless rave reviews from the media. In March 2012, after picking up Palace's Young Player of the Year award in consecutive seasons, he was voted the Football League's Young Player of the Year. Later that year, having already played for England at Under-19 and Under-21 level, Zaha won his first full international cap for his country, when he came off the bench in a friendly international against Sweden.

Soon, the Premiership big-guns began to circle Palace's prized asset, with Manchester United finally winning the race for his signature for a fee reported to be in the region £15 million, although part of the deal was that Zaha was immediately loaned back to Palace for the remainder of the season, to aid their promotion challenge. The arrangement certainly paid dividends for Palace as Zaha inspired the Eagles' return the top flight by scoring two goals in a dramatic

ZAHA

Play-Off semi-final second leg victory over Brighton & Hove Albion to take his club to Wembley and then, in the final against Watford, he won what turned out to be the match-winning penalty.

Zaha's first competitive game for Manchester United also saw him pick up his first major honour at club level, when he played in the 2-0 victory over Wigan Athletic in the 2013 FA Community Shield at Wembley. His first-team opportunities at United were limited and in January 2014 he joined Cardiff City on loan until the end of the season.

Then in August 2014, he signed for Palace again on loan and celebrated his return by netting a dramatic last-minute equaliser in a 3-3 draw against Newcastle United at St James' Park.

To the delight of Palace fans, Zaha's move to Selhurst Park was made permanent during the January 2015 transfer window and he is now a key member of Alan Pardew's Premier League squad.

SOUTH
LONDON
AND
PROUD